"I," PERIOD.

"I," PERIOD.

MELISSA McCURRY-PORTER

Cover concept by Justin Anderson, Xclusive Image, Stone Mountain, Georgia.

ISBN 1-58597-377-7

Library of Congress Control Number: 2005937973

LEATHERS PUBLISHING

4500 College Boulevard
Overland Park, KS 66211
888-888-7696
www.leatherspublishing.com

Dedicated to my son, Xavier Michael Porter.
You are my star, "Sweet-Pumpkin."

Acknowledgments

LORD, THANK YOU! I did not have a miscarriage nor a stillbirth. I brought this baby (book) to full term only because You put me in the trenches and covered me with Your grace and mercy. I, along with my children's children, am forever indebted to you, Lord Jesus Christ our Savior, who has blessed my soul and trusted me with Your gracious spirit. Without You, Lord, I am nothing; only through you do I "LIVE!" Thank You, for You are so wondrous and so worthy to be praised.

Mommy and Daddy, I'm sorry, but I have to say it – I have the best parents on the face of this earth. Your love alone endures all. Thank you for raising me up, teaching and showing me the way. Sometimes letting me go and do "my own thing," but only because of your wisdom has it made me who I am today. Thank you!

Grandmother Victoria Williams – you are truly my hero; your strength is unbelievable. You gave birth to 10 children who then blessed you with numerous grandchildren, all who love you so much. Thank you, Grandma. I am who I am today because I wanted to be like you! Rest in peace, R.B. Williams.

My sister, Michelle – I can write a book on you alone, your undying love and willingness to always please and do good by others. It will pay off for you! It is not in vain. I have always looked up to my beautiful sister. Thanks for being the best sister anyone could ever have, even when I was a brat. I love you, Chris and Ali "Sug-Sug."

To my brother, Derrick, and my sister, Jessica McCurry – what's up? The Lord gave you to our family, and I love you so much! Do your big sister a favor: be good and do well in all that you set out to do. Don't ever let anyone deter you from your goals. I am so proud of you both!

To Pastor and Loretta Jones – I am so glad the Lord loves us! You both are an inspiration to me! Take care of those boys and that little lady. I am still reflecting on Joshua's song that Jesus "gave him" for the family reunion. WONDERFUL!

Thank you, Aunt Splo. It was you who introduced me as a child to different things that have allowed me to always be open. Everything and everybody deserves at least a chance. Thank you! Rest in peace, Geo.

To all of my family, too many to name, but please know that each of you holds a special place in my heart! I would not trade my family for the world. I love you!

To my best friend, Marlo Hawthorne-Darrington – it seems like yesterday when we met and became friends in the sixth grade. Although the teachers always asked me, "Why do you hang around her? She's bad!" I always knew your heart was a heart of gold. Thank you for the inspiration and the encouragement you have given me throughout the years; it is truly irreplaceable. I wish you much joy and success, all that your heart desires. Stay true to yourself. You are a beautiful butterfly.

To my friend, Terrhonda Hillman – the Lord only knows this book would not be here without you and your encouragement. "Thanks" isn't enough to say! I will never forget the day I told you, "Girl, I think I need to go to the hospital, I am losing my mind." You told me, "Girl, please, you are fine." You "saved" me from going insane. I cried so many days, and you were there on the crucial ones! I dedicate this book to you as well – you helped me bring forth the birth of this book and you went through the birthing pains with me! I love you!

To Shirley and Kenneth Borden – it has never been about

me or you; it has always been about my son's destiny. I cannot say thank you enough for taking great care of my baby boy. Every time Xavier breaks out in a song about Jesus, I can't help but smile and think about "Mrs. Shirley." I love you. Thank you for helping me mature in more ways than one. You will definitely be missed; you know you will have to follow Xavier to "big kids school." Please stay close.

To my spiritual daddy, Bishop Eddie Long – I look at you week after week and my love for you grows. Your undying love for the Lord, your strength, your endurance, your attitude, your willingness to give of yourself is uncanny. Thank you for MAKING my spirit see more clearly through the word of the Lord.

To my friends, Chonita, Lynn, Kim, Ubi, Nikita, Travonda, Mauri, Carla, Vivian, Jeffrey, DeCarlos, Bobo and Randy – I can remember each one of you vividly and look back with a smile. My memories of the good times we shared can never be erased or replaced. I hope each of you can at least take away one blessing in this book. WE KICKED IT! "Much Love." Randy, I believe you now: I think everybody's gone crazy.

Tracy Shirley, you are irreplaceable, no need to say more. Love you, "Sexy T."

A special "thank you" goes out to all my Atlanta family and friends. Although I have not named you individually, trust that you hold a special place in my heart for making ATL my home away from home.

To my Porter and Miami families – thanks for all the love, acceptance and happy times you gave me. God bless and keep each of you! Nita, Freeda, Linda, Cashmier (Boochy) – y'all are my folks; love you! Thank you, Momma Reeda and Daddy Arthur Porter. Thanks, A.J.

And, last but not least, THANK YOU, Arthur Porter, for

MAKING me grow. I was truly a babe when I met you, and through you I became a woman full of overflowing knowledge. We experienced so much over the years, but unbeknownst to us, it was all part of the plan. Your wisdom is a gift. I wish you all the joy that your heart desires. Thank you for our son.

Foreword

TO EVERYTHING THERE is a season and a time for every purpose under the sun. You are proof positive that our Lord and Savior is always with us and He will forever direct us in all our ways. He is the light that shines in the darkness. We cannot see Him, but He has spoken through your faithful voice. We cannot feel Him, but He is the power at work in our lives. He is assurance; He is peace in times of uncertainness. He is always there for us! At times we may fail to find Him — but he always finds us. Our faith in Him is sometimes unsure — His faith in us never waivers. He knows our heart and he feels our pain. HE LOVES US!

What an honor being asked to write the Foreword for your book. I congratulate you on your accomplishment, as well as your willingness to share with others your life's lessons. You have done a wonderful job sharing the heartaches experienced in your life or foreseen in the lives of others. You have not played the blame game. The steps you used for helping to create a better life, not only for yourself but also for other women, is a gift that you not only have received, but that you're willing to share in hopes of enriching the lives of others. Having recognized the problems encountered in your own life and through your pain, having demonstrated a dedication to others like yourself who are also having life-changing experiences, you will be blessed by your willingness to share the steps necessary to change their lives for the better.

To God be the glory!

— Patricia Pierson

Contents

Introduction

WHEN I TURNED 30 years old, I was ecstatic. I really couldn't understand my excitement that I was joining the 30-and-up crew, but now I realize I was entering a new phase of my life, and with anything new it's an exciting time.

I'll never forget, I prematurely celebrated my birthday with two strangers while traveling on an airplane to my hometown. One of the individuals traveled frequently, and it was the first air flight for the other gentleman. The guy who had never flown before was nervous about flying, especially after September 11th, but we reassured him that everything would be fine. The frequent flyer spoke out of experience, but I spoke and reassured him that I was on the plane and my 30th birthday was coming up in a few days and it was not my time, I was sure of that. I believed God had something in store for me.

We all talked and enjoyed the flight; before long the guy settled down. At that very point of my life I made up my mind that life is for the living. I began to live mentally.

I was in the middle of putting my life back together after a separation from my husband. I literally thought it was the end of my world. I would later realize it really was not the end, but the beginning of a new era of my life! I sure had my good days along with the bad days to follow, but I remembered the vow I made to myself: "Life is for the living." The minutes, the days, the months got easier only because I knew God was taking me somewhere. I never knew what I would have to endure mentally to eventually find peace within.

While reading this book, you may or may not be experiencing any heartaches. It may be the encouragement you need for your life to move forward, or maybe just a little heartfelt inspiration. Whatever the case may be, understand this book was placed in my spirit from God to show myself, along with other women, that you are not alone even when you are physically alone. Your trials are ONLY for a season, yet ALWAYS for a reason! Please check your attitude, your ego, along with your opinions at the door and leave them! It is imperative that you read the entire book from beginning to end.

Although I really didn't have a clue what God was doing in my life, I began to thank Him, and I celebrated the trials I was experiencing. (That was hard to do.) I began to understand that my reward would be great and it is – the birth of this book to my sisters. This book goes out to all of those who are wondering, "What in the hell is going on in my life?", and those who are saying, "Absolutely nothing is going on in my life," as well as to those wanting to give up. All I have to say is, "Be patient; don't give up; there is so much in store for you!"

I don't even know you, and I KNOW that you have a purpose. I pray just by you picking up this book and reading it that you will realize your purpose. As I had to, you must come to the realization that everything in your life starts with *"I," Period.* This is not the selfish "I," but the "I" that says, "I will make a difference in my home, in my family, in my community, in my church, in my workplace. Wherever 'I' am, 'I' will make a difference! I will not wait for someone else to change for me to experience happiness; I understand that true happiness starts from within."

The Preface and the Afterword are two poems that I wrote a few years ago when I had no clue of what God was birthing in me. I did not even know I had the talent of writing. God will always give you clips of what's going on or what is about to transpire in your life; it is up to you to walk it out!

Our life is like a jigsaw puzzle – we have all the pieces we need, we just have to arrange them in their proper places. Just like a puzzle, we try different pieces that don't work; we try and try until we find the piece that fits perfectly. When you start a puzzle, it looks virtually impossible, but when you are finished, you look at it and say, "Wow, who would have imagined all those little pieces make up this big picture?" The same goes for our lives – when we start living out our purpose, we say, "Who would have imagined?"

When you are finished reading this book, I want you to get a jigsaw puzzle, not an easy one but a difficult one, and put it together to prepare yourself mentally. After you have finished, start working on your own puzzle (YOUR LIFE!).

Endure (and enjoy) the process!

Preface

GET OFF THAT 9

So you say you have never loved like this before,
The ones that were before me never experienced you to this degree.
Always the playa, the shot calla and nonetheless the balla.
So I come into yo' life and my love has got you hypnotized,
Where you can't see, only want to taste me,
only want to be with me, not without me, only want to smell, smell my sweet scent.
It sends yo' mind so far in the clouds that I have to say,
"Hey, hey, can you come down off that 9?"
You tell me, you don't know what it is about me got you so mesmerized,
The other girls are callin' and you say all I want is my "Sweet Melissa,"
Check you la-ta. Huh is what they say, she must get you fee-ning.
As you give me all the attention I desire,
Make me feel like I am queen, queen of the Nile,
Love me like none other; make me feel like this is true, this is the one,
The one that my God has sent to be my king.
So I give in return all the love that I am.

And you say,
"Hey, hey, can you come down off that 9?"
Yeah , I must be sprung, no more late night calls sayin', I'm coming through to see you,
Thinkin' 'bout havin' babies,
Rearranging my life, makin' plans for only you!
Yeah this is the one.
I hear wedding bells; I'm walkin' down the aisle.
I am fine. Not a soul can tell me a thing 'bout me or my king.
The days roll by and the babies come.
It's all a dream in this fairy tale life or so it seems.
I call your cell, there's no answer at FO' in the morn, where in the hell can you be?
It turns into five, then six, six-thirty in the freakin' morning.
You must be losing yo' mind to stroll in my castle like yo' stuff-don't-stink.
There are no lies that I want to hear.
When I heard you say,
"Hey, hey, can you come down off that 9?"
I should have ran, ran so farrrr, sooo fast, but love had me wrapped.
I could not see the game that you ran on me.
Yeah, I was queen fo' a day;
but once my love was strong like a cup of black coffee.
You were gone in the wind. Had conquered me.
It was a challenge like you never knew.
The last thing I heard was, "I'm gone be a nigga fo' life."
Huh, that's funny 'cause I confused you with my king.

Chapter 1

THE FAIRY TALE

"OKAY, I WILL be the mommy and you will be the daddy, but first we have to get married, and then you have to go out and get a job to take care of me and our baby." I can still remember the puzzled look on my playmate's face, as if to say, "You are crazy!" But, of course, he always went along with whatever I wanted to play because, as I would later find out, women have the ability to get a man to do just about whatever they want; they just have to know how! From the beginning of time, women were given the natural ability to hypnotize men with their beauty and charm, leaving them speechless and spellbound (to say the least). But something has happened along the way — women and men have grown so far apart that it's actually killing us both. The only way we can put our genuine God-given relationships back together is by starting with ourselves and working outward.

As little girls growing up, we are filled with this great big fairy tale of getting married and living happily ever after. Unfortunately, we are clueless as to how this happily ever after is really going to happen. No one sits us down to tell us how to have a successful marriage. Even if someone does try to talk to us about marriage, we really don't listen, because the fairy tale of marriage is so vivid in our imaginations that we throw all the information out the window and live by what has been instilled in us since childhood. All we know is that mommies and daddies get married and then have babies. We really don't see what goes on behind closed doors. We just know that we go to the grocery store and get food, the lights just magically go on and off, the car runs off gas from the gas station, Santa Claus brings lots and lots of presents, the Easter bunny brings an Easter basket, Mommy and Daddy buy presents for our birthdays, the ATM machine spits out money at will, and if you were fortunate like me, when a tooth fell out the Tooth-Fairy would always bring you a quarter.

Yes, Daddy's favorite quote was, "You think money grows on trees." I knew that it didn't, "only" because leaves grew on trees. After thinking about it, I was really oblivious as to how hard Mommy and Daddy actually worked so I could live in this "fairy tale" world. I knew that my parents always argued about money and never having enough, as well as other issues, but I never knew their marriage would ultimately end due to all the drama surrounding our lives — because of all the expectations that had not been lived up to, all the disappointments of what was supposed to be, and finally all the lies to make things better.

I always just closed my door and continued to plan my wedding with Prince Charming. Who would I be today? Cinderella? My prince would take me away from all this chaos to live in a faraway castle and everyone would adore me. Or when I got in my bed I would be Sleeping Beauty and fall off to sleep and dream of my prince kissing me so sweetly, like I was the only girl in the world. Maybe Snow White? We all know her prince kissed her back to life. How about Rapunzel? The only thing she had to do to get her man was let down her golden hair. Wouldn't it be wonderful if life were really that simple? As little girls growing up, we read these fairy tales over and over again; the memories of these tales are etched into our thought processes. We start to incorporate fairy tales into our lives. Before we know it, we have built in our minds this dream guy, this dream wedding and this dream lifestyle. The only thing missing in these fairy tales is the drama that is inevitable in real life. Something drastic almost always has to occur in our lives to make us wake up and smell the coffee.

How do we prepare ourselves for something that really doesn't exist in our mind or imagination, you might ask? Yes, I heard Mommy and Daddy argue, but I would always say to myself, "That's not going to be my husband and me because we are going to love each other too much to argue" — end of story.

I myself would later be faced with the realization of finding out that marriage is much more complicated than just being in love. I would find that it takes two people willing to make sacrifices about their ideas and opinions in order to come to terms with someone else's thoughts and emotions. When you choose to marry a person for life, it is no longer about "you" and how "you" feel about a particular situation; it is about how "we" feel. The hardest part of this equation is that, no matter how much you think you have in common with another human being, you are never going to agree 100% on everything. Then comes the drama, because whose ideas are right? No one wants to back down!

Throughout this book I will explore the reasons why women are continuously trying to find a self-fulfilled life and looking in all the wrong places to do so. We will learn to truly believe and understand that self-fulfillment starts within "your" heart and "your" mind. You have to be able to give yourself joy in order to truly accept and appreciate the life you have been given. While reading this book, you may feel a strong sense of, "It's just not fair," but it's not about being fair; it's about taking responsibility for you and your actions, end, period, point blank — taking a look at why you end up in positions that make you feel as if your life is being turned inside out. By no means is this a book to down women or make them feel less important or less valuable. It is just the opposite; this is a book to let you know that you are great, no matter what has occurred throughout your life, no matter how many mistakes you have made or think you have made, no matter how old you are. YOU ARE GREAT! Let's explore the possibilities.

This is also a book intended to help you gain some knowledge of why you are not getting what you truly desire out of life, moving you outside the fairy tale world. By the end of this book, I predict that you will be a better judge of character about what "really" matters in life, your life in particular. Over the last few decades, the tables have turned tremendously from our grandmothers' times, but are we any more successful at life than they were? I don't believe we are; although we have far more material possessions than they had, we are failing miserably at life. Ask yourself these important questions, and go into this book with an open mind that you WANT to change. You may not believe you NEED to change, but trust me, we all have room for improvement.

I, too, am a woman who has experienced pain and the ups and downs of life and love. Yet I finally understood that I couldn't continue down the same path of incompleteness and unfulfillment over and over again if joy truly was to be the most essential part of the life that I was seeking and searching after.

Open up your mind and explore all the parts that are dark and have no true understanding. When I say dark, discover the areas where there seem to be missing pieces and you don't quite know what the missing pieces are. Places deep in your thoughts, where you really don't want to go because of the pain. Open the door of your mind to step into a new, refreshing, self-assured, fun-loving and meaningful life. We only have one life to live! So why not live the only one you have and make the best of it?!

Chapter 2

LEARNING TO LOVE YOURSELF

WOMEN TEND TO always look for someone to tell us how beautiful we are or how great we could actually be. We don't realize how important it is to feel good about ourselves and treat ourselves well. If someone else chooses to love and appreciate you, you have to look at it as being icing on the cake.

We first have to define the word "good" before we can begin to understand what is lacking in our lives. Our word "good" can easily be defined as anything positive in life that challenges you to grow. *Webster's Dictionary* refers to "good" as "better or best," and goes on to give the definition as having desirable, favorable, suitable, virtuous, full, whole, superior to average, competent, valid, ample, bountiful, pleasant, appropriate or beneficial qualities.

These definitions are all positive attributes that need to be reflected by us in our lives. If our lives are not a representation of some, if not all, of these definitions, we need to look on the inside and find out what we are missing in order to start fulfilling ourselves and our lives! Once we have determined if we possess these "good" qualities or even if there is not one to be found, we must be willing to observe our behavior from a standpoint of determining whether our life is working for us or working against us. Once we start self-observing, we are better equipped to handle the pain as well as the truth.

Believe it or not, everyone goes through a period in his or her life when they wake up and say, "What is my purpose in life?", and then turn over and grasp the pillow to say to ourselves, (or we may even yell it out loud), "I don't have a purpose. I don't even know why I'm here!" This is okay because once we start to sink into what I call a "THINK TANK," we find ourselves really taking time to try and find ourselves and what is missing in our lives.

When we are in this "Think Tank," no one really knows what to say to us because everyone's struggle is different. What may be important to you may be just the opposite for someone else. So when you start to speak, even the closest person to you may say, "What are you talking about, what are you going through?" It seems as if you are in a foreign country speaking an unknown language. You feel like you are in this "Think Tank" alone with barely enough air to breathe to continue battling through "LIFE!"

What you don't know is that you are in a foreign country, you have never been "here" before, and if you did, you only visited. You didn't take up residence because you didn't like the feel of this "place." Before, you could resort to your fairy tale life or call your best girlfriend or most likely your mother because she always knows what to say. Not while in the "Think Tank!" No one feels your pain; so it seems. Life seems to be moving, but you're not moving along with it because you don't know which roads to take. You almost want to give up, if you haven't already. Your whole life feels like a great big ball of confusion.

When you start to feel overwhelmed by life or your ordeals, or you can't turn around, you have to keep moving! Moving where? Moving further into the depths of understating, searching after the answers for your life and your life goals. The answers will unravel once you start searching after understanding. You may feel quite frankly like you are putting a great big jigsaw puzzle together, and life itself can be mirrored as such.

Fathom this: before you are born, your puzzle of life is all together, and then as you grow and live, that perfect puzzle comes undone. When you finally realize that your puzzle, "Life," is "mixed up," then you have to find a way to put the proper pieces back in their respective places. This is the challenge because we have so many aspects of life that must be taken into consideration. We scramble around desperately trying to figure our lives out! The utter lack of hope sends us into a moment of despair that we will do anything to "make our lives work," almost always moving us in the wrong direction.

While in the "Think Tank," it seems as if you are walking through a maze with no clue as to how to get out. But don't stop and panic; you must move on. While in the "Think Tank," it is imperative to believe there is a light at the end of the tunnel. Think of it as a test. Like any other test, you must be prepared; you have to have studied this thing called life in order to pass the test. The only way you can do this is to keep your eyes and ears open to your surroundings. Don't take people and things for granted. Listen to older, wiser people around you who have climbed many mountains and have stories of success, along with stories of failure, to guide you as well as encourage you to keep going. One of the biggest problems we experience in life is that there are no sample tests, only trials and tribulations to ensure that you will at least score a passing grade. You only fail when you give up and quit! Moving forward in life gives us the opportunity to increase our score (wisdom).

Haven't you heard the old saying, "Try and try again"? If something is not working for you in your life, try a different route. Don't get discouraged and throw your hands up and say, "I give!" We often find ourselves asking why life is so hard. But what have you found to be easy that is worth having? You must learn to appreciate yourself and demand that others appreciate you just as much. Life is TOO HARD to let others run over you with no consideration. What are you working so hard for, if you will allow others to use you as a doormat?

Ladies, this is not an excuse to be nasty or cocky to others because you feel they "owe you something." Appreciation should be a prerequisite for someone to be ALLOWED the opportunity to be a part of your life. However, let's keep it real; you are only a pleasure to be around if you are radiating in the qualities of "GOOD", that we addressed earlier.

Let's study this for a moment (life, that is). Life is so indescribable – there are a million different emotions associated with life, ranging from phenomenal to earth-shattering and everything in-between. We are conditioned from birth to depend on another human life for survival, unaware that God has planted our footsteps. It's up to us to dig ourselves out and grow into what God has called us to be. This is easier said than done, because while we have been conditioned to be dependent on other humans for survival, we almost get lost in finding ourselves. We put on facades to mask our fears and insecurities because we are always pretending to be something we really are not. We keep passing the "Think Tank" because it's scary! It's scary to be alone. As soon as we start finding ourselves alone, we run out and find someone new who can possibly calm the fears and insecurities we face. Soon they are gone, too.

This may happen a couple of times, where people or things seem to be here today and gone tomorrow. Then maybe after a million more times it feels like the "Think Tank" finally catches you and won't release you until you at least have captured the understanding that you have to go through your trials and tribulations, not around them, in order to get some understanding in your life. Once you have this concept down, you may be able to possibly score more than a passing grade. It's not the grade that really matters; it's your willingness to seek a higher level of wisdom, strength and understanding in your life that counts.

While in the "Think Tank," you start to hear your spirit whispering to your heart. You hear your spirit all the time trying to speak to you; yet you have never listened quite so attentively, and it's telling you something you probably never heard before, or if you did, you really didn't believe it. Your spirit is telling you that you ARE beautiful, you ARE wonderful, and you ARE great. It makes you smile, and you find yourself feeling like you are five years old again. A little shy, but confident that you ARE beautiful, wonderful and great, which you discovered all by yourself. You find yourself waking up ahead of the alarm clock ready to tackle the day, wanting to take advantage of all that life has to offer. You start to make plans for your life based on what you have decided is needed to make you happy and proud of yourself. You're on cloud nine. You feel in control of your life, and this is the way it is supposed to be.

Wait! Here comes the "but" ... with maturity and challenges come bigger and greater challenges. But that's okay because you still have the number one rule under your belt. You must go through your trials and tribulations, not around them, no matter how unfamiliar the territory may be. This is just a part of life – waiting for the next challenge and knowing and believing that it's a winnable game. Give yourself time to process the challenge because it will be difficult, to say the least. You don't have to be Superwoman, so don't pretend you are. Determine what you are up against and map out how you are going to handle the ordeal. You must come to the belief that this situation is only put before you to make you a stronger person mentally, emotionally and perhaps even physically, moving you into a new arena of your life.

Neither I nor anyone else can tell you exactly how to handle your situation, but one important thing you must do is stand firm on the decisions you do make. Whatever outcome arises from it, take responsibility and live with it. Don't go run and hide under the bed and cry out, "I can't take this!" YES YOU CAN! Do put on your armor and get ready to win a battle. Why give up in the middle of the puzzle before you see how it turns out? Believing in yourself is a vital part of life, and learning to love yourself for who you are is even more important. Remember, you only have one life to live, so live it well with meaning and great endurance. The "Think Tank" is only for a season, yet always for a reason, but remember – seasons always change!

Chapter 3

STOP WASTING YOUR TIME

DO YOU KNOW that tomorrow is not promised? Luckily, it isn't because procrastination would become a way of life. We would always think about what we could put off until later, or we would say things like, "I have time," and you know what would happen? Nothing! Absolutely nothing would ever get accomplished because we would always feel like we have time. We would waste more time than we already do. I believe God knew this, so he gave us a deadline, called "Life and Death," but He managed to leave one vital thing out: when our life would end. No one's days are promised, and no one knows when they will meet their Maker, so that's why we must make the best out of every minute of every day we have here on earth.

What are your dreams and your desires? Do you even have dreams? Don't worry if nothing comes to mind. Until I started writing this book, I was searching for my purpose. I wasn't content with myself because I knew I had a purpose, but I wasn't quite sure what my purpose was. I was looking at everybody around me, and there were all types of talent. I started brainstorming and narrowing my purpose or my talent down. I was like, "Okay, I can't sing, dance or act, so I guess I won't be some type of superstar." Those three things were out. Although I wanted to be an actress, there was no passion. I was just searching for something — anything. I'm no Einstein, so inventing something was out, but I failed to realize you don't have to be a genius to come up with a great idea or concept. You just have to be determined and focused and believe in yourself and your idea. I found myself trying to find something that I was put on this earth to do, but nothing was coming to mind. I did, however, know that I wanted to counsel and help women, but when my life started turning upside down, I didn't know how the heck I could help someone else when I felt my own life was in shambles.

This may sound a little out there, but as I told myself, my astrological sign is Pisces and we are supposed to be creative people, yet where is my creativity? I have none! I was almost ready to give up hope and settle for just working the rest of my life. I continued being restless, but I also continued to listen to my Bishop preach, "Don't die without ever living your life." My spirit was yearning for something more out of life. I started writing to settle my thoughts, and after I finished writing, I would have a clear train of thought and a sense of peace.

One day I wrote a letter to my friend because I needed to get some "stuff" off my chest. Later, she came back to me and said, "Let's write a book." I said, "Who? You!" This was her gift, her talent; although it wasn't being pursued, I might add. She was good, really good, creative and passionate about writing, but not me! I felt writing was a way to get my head clear. I really didn't take my friend seriously because

I didn't have any confidence about writing. But I thought, what do I have to lose? Nothing or everything, depending on how you look at it. So I sat down one night and just started writing about why I felt women have such a fairy tale way of living. When the first chapter was complete, I said to myself, "Wow! This is good." I was surprised. I was surprised because I was creative. I was creative enough to think about my thoughts and emotions and put them down on paper and make a storyline for someone to be interested enough to want to follow. After I wrote that first chapter, I gained confidence that, "Hmm, maybe I have something here."

I continued to write and finally started feeling passionate about something I was doing. I found myself getting discouraged and I would tell myself things like, "You are no writer. How do you think you can stand up to all those other great authors who have sold millions of books?" When I felt discouraged, I did something that I never thought I would do. I shared my work with people in my life, to get their opinions. I wanted to get a response on what I had written so far, to see if I was on the right track and to see if my writing made sense to others. I wanted to know if I needed to be awakened from my dream.

The feedback came back very positive and encouraging. The encouragement was important for me because I had never really done anything that I could claim or be proud of. At this point I was no longer discouraged about living up to other writers' expectations. I wanted to write for me; I felt a comfort zone. I gained a sense that if this book does not sell one copy, I would still be proud of my accomplishment. That was a huge statement for me because I was always expecting a return for my hard work.

This leads me to my point: STOP WASTING YOUR TIME! It's so funny because we feel like we don't have a life or any business of our own, so we try to get in everyone else's. You do have a life and you do have some business; you just have to find it. Sometimes the search is long and hard, but trust me, it's there, and it's worth the search.

Why do we spend countless hours reading the latest magazines or tabloids to find out who is marrying who and who is divorcing who? How much money someone other than ourselves is making or what the latest hairstyles are? How many times do we have to watch the same music video to get the picture? I know reading magazines and watching television is a form of entertainment, but it is a huge distraction. It pulls our attention away from what we should be focusing on and makes us lazy – yes, lazy – and keeps us from getting our own lives in check. We are too busy fantasizing about someone else's accomplishments. After obsessively watching other people's successful lives, their huge accomplishments, we get intimidated and say, "That could never be me." Why couldn't it? We are all human. You just have to be determined and have will power.

Will power is strong because it takes a lot of inner strength. It is so easy to do nothing and be content with just making ends meet. You don't have to live life with the frustration of collecting a paycheck every week or two that's going to be gone by the time the next payday rolls around. You have to first make a personal stand that you are going to do it. You may or may not know what "IT" is that you are going to do, but the key is, you do know you are not going to be in this rut all your life and you want something better for you and your family. That's an important start!

Once you have the will power and determination to make something happen in your life, things will start to happen. Things are not happening by chance; they are happening because you are actually making a stand to make them happen. How can you get a good job when you sit on the couch every day watching television? The job is not going to knock on your door. You are the one who has to do the knocking. After you get the good job, how do you think you're going to get the promotion if you do just enough to collect a check? You have to go beyond the call of duty and convince your superiors that you are worthy of advancement. After you get the promotion, where do you go from there? It's unlimited because now you have knowledge; the only thing that limits you is yourself.

Fear plays a big role in this because we are afraid that if we step out on faith we could possibly fail. Did you just read what I just said? Could possibly fail! Flip it over and say, could possibly succeed! Fear makes us look at the negative side of situations instead of looking at the positive side. But what about common sense, I hear someone asking? How could we live without common sense? It wouldn't be much fun. Common sense is important and is actually required in a successful life. For example, once you get the promotion, (which, of course, comes with a bigger paycheck), don't go out and purchase a bigger home, car, clothes or something material. Put the money into something that is able to give you a return. Once you step out on faith, you will have a little cushion to back you up and get you through the intermediate period.

It's all about continuing education; no matter what you are educating yourself on, it's the never-ending desire to learn more that's important! Don't ever think you have enough knowledge because that's when you start to fail. The world is ever-changing. You have to be able to change your mind! Sometimes things change because too many people have too much knowledge about a matter that once only a few people had knowledge on. So believe that the rules are going to change at some point in time and probably after you just got the rules down pat. The key is to be one step ahead of the game; don't get content with where you are. Start investing in your future. This was a very valuable lesson I read from the book entitled *Who Moved My Cheese?* Think about it — if you have been working at a job for say 10 years and you go to work and the doors are locked with no explanation, what are you going to do? Cry? But if you have something else that you have been pursuing, it's not so traumatizing because you have something to fall back on.

The world we live in now is very shaky; I really don't think people realize what we are in for. Every day that we are given the grace to wake up is valuable; we don't have time to waste our energy on frivolous activities, or people for that matter. If you have some ideas, start putting them into motion. Get a game plan, surround yourself with people who have similar ideas, or at least with people who are motivated. When we are around negative people or people who aren't motivated, they tend to rob us of our full potential, either intentionally or unintentionally, by telling us what we're trying to accomplish is impossible. Don't believe this; anything is possible. Do allow yourself to be open to constructive criticism only from people who have either been where you are trying to go or from people who are motivated to go somewhere.

One thing that you must realize is that you will get discouraged because you are going to have your good days and your bad days. But when you find yourself getting discouraged, just take a look at where you used to be and how much you have accomplished. It may be mentally or physically small or large, but the important fact is your willingness to want to change and grow!

Let me take a station break and tell you about something that happened to me while I was in the middle of writing this book. I went to JAIL. Yes, I did. You want to know why? I went to jail for a speeding ticket from five years ago that had been paid. And you want to know why I was pulled over in the first place? Can you guess — speeding? I was informed that I had failed to appear in court for the five-year-old violation, but I knew that I had; I remembered everything like it was yesterday — even what happened when I appeared before the judge. You want to know something else? I had an updated clearance letter from the Department of Motor Vehicles stating that I had no outstanding tickets or warrants and my license was supposedly "clean." I sat in jail for 16 hours (going through the system) because of someone's mistake. I was very upset by what I was facing, but I did one important thing. I chose to get better instead of getting bitter; this was hard, to say the least. I blamed myself. I should have not been speeding in the first place is what I told myself. While sitting in jail, I took a mental note of my surroundings and the goals that I was currently trying to accomplish. I looked at the women around me who were so broken for one reason or another. I kept telling myself there is a reason for me being here today; there is a purpose. I spoke briefly to the women, asking why they were jailed and, unfortunately, found a lot of denial. It was everyone else's fault other than the women themselves as to why they were jailed. I got reasons like: "My boyfriend did such and such, so I retaliated;" "I was driving on a suspended license, but the cop was just picking on me." There was a list of stories from these women about their incarcerations, but none of the women I talked to seem to accept responsibility in trying to find a solution to their problems.

I began to look at my life and my issues and told myself I needed to get a grip and stop complaining and stop throwing myself a pity party because my life could be much worse. I could have made one wrong turn and been on the same path as so many women of the world today. All it takes is one mistake and your whole life could be turned upside down. Don't fool yourself into believing for one second that you are any better than the next person and your life is exempt from the harsh realities of this world, because it is not. We as woman need to start recognizing that our sisters' problems are all of our problems and go above and beyond to do something about helping them instead of hurting them. We have to stop turning our noses up at our neighbor because they are not as fortunate as we are or they don't look the part. That's what most of us are doing anyway — "looking the part." But when you take away the fancy clothes, expensive cars and flashy jewelry, it's scary what you might find implanted in the hearts of some women who are simply clueless when it comes to real life.

As I was leaving my unfortunate event, I waved goodbye to the women I had spent the last hours with. I had tears in my eyes because I had found my purpose. My purpose was to continue writing this book. SO MANY women need it. My purpose is to write to women about women, about where we have been for so long and where we are headed. It is important to realize that you are important and you do have a purpose in life, regardless of what someone may have told you. Most importantly, we have to start accepting responsibility for our own actions. Oddly, the sad part of the matter is I really don't think we have ever been taught how to accept responsibility for our actions – accepting responsibility to the point that it becomes an effective part of our internal growth process, admitting and realizing our downfalls and mistakes. It is so much easier to blame someone else for our problems and not feel as if we have made mistakes; it actually makes us feel better if we are not to blame. We don't want to believe that sort of behavior actually exists in our brain. More importantly, we don't realize that sometimes we comprehend things differently to make ourselves "feel better." We are naïve to the fact that we are not looking at our own actions to see what key roles we played to get ourselves caught up in the unfortunate events of our lives. We seem to notice only the part where someone else entered our life and challenge the fact that's where the problems began. Unfortunately, in most cases that's not the beginning of the problem or even the end of the problem.

To give you an example, as a child you may have been

subject to seeing your mother involved in bad relationships; you may have witnessed your mother constantly being mistreated by men. Unknowingly to you, you grow up with a preconceived notion that all men are dogs and will treat women badly. You go into relationships not trusting men because of your childhood experiences. You take these memories into your adulthood. You soon become accustomed to going in and out of relationships and attribute your pitfalls to meeting no-good men. Unfortunately, what you don't realize is this was not the beginning of your problem. The problem started when you unconsciously went into the relationship thinking all men are dogs and treat women badly. The problems spiraled downhill from there. You had no clue that what you experienced as a child could possibly have anything to do with your adult life experiences. It's easier to think and feel you met the wrong person and he was just a dog. That may work the first couple of times, but about "the 50th" relationship, you must begin to accept responsibility and do something about improving your life standards.

After my trying day, it took me a few days to get motivated and back on track of writing. I had to put my thoughts into perspective; I really wanted this to be a good book. I realized that women really have some issues that need to be faced and addressed. I wanted this book to be something with meaning and substance that would be able to touch the hearts of the readers. I have read a lot of "self-help" books and have come away with a new sense of self, but I felt the books were too easy on me. The books that I had encountered never made me look at the reasons why things occurred the way they did in my life. The books almost never informed me that I was wasting valuable time and energy or pointed me in the right direction. They almost never informed me that personal responsibility was vital, and if I didn't take responsibility for my own actions, I might as well throw all the other positives out the window.

Being positive is one essential step; however, if you don't realize you have to be accountable for your own actions, it's no good. I would be on the road to success and excited about my newfound thoughts and opinions, but something was definitely missing. I usually found myself slowly drifting back to my comfortable level of thinking. In most cases, you have to practically transform your whole entire thought process in order for change to actually occur. You have to be able to recognize that your old way of thinking has not worked for you thus far, so why continue on the same path?

I want to show my readers that you are not alone. Women from all walks of life are going through a battle of not knowing their purpose and are walking through life lost! If you don't think you have a purpose, think again, because you do. Start brainstorming. Look at your life and some of your talents. Some of your ideas can be very minute, but look at them anyway. Remember, greatness begins with a single thought. Stop playing the victim of your past ordeals and put them out of your mind. Stop blaming other people for your trials and tribulations. Stop wasting your time bickering with people who are before you to distract you. Stop wasting your time fighting battles that are not worth the time of day. You could be using your time gaining ground instead of losing ground. I know it's very hard to let things go when you feel someone is taking advantage of you, but trust me, it's not worth it.

Women spend a great deal of time battling with men or people in general to prove they are not naïve and are strong. Women hate to feel like someone is taking advantage of them; they feel like they are smarter and tougher than that. A lot of times we say things only to prove to someone that we are up on their "games." Question: If you are up on their "games" and if you feel they are trying to pull the wool over your eyes, why are you still dealing with them? I hear someone say, "Oh, but I love him." Yes, love is a valid reason; I won't dispute that, but is it worth your heartache? We all take "stuff" off people that perhaps another person would not, but when you constantly find yourself battling for reasons that you are really oblivious to, take note – another word for oblivious is ignorant. I was trying to put it mildly, for those of us who need to be spoon-fed. But just so you know it's really ignorance that keeps us bound, may I say it again: STOP WASTING YOUR TIME! If someone is not putting forth the energy and the effort that you need, move forward. We need people around us who are going to encourage us to do better, not those who are going to hinder us from living life and living it more abundantly.

Again, don't get discouraged if you really don't have a game plan right this very minute. But start today! Start looking for who you are and what you were put on the earth to accomplish, because your life is too valuable to waste and let it pass you by. I assure you, time waits on no one! REMEMBER, we only have one life to live, so take advantage of every opportunity given.

Chapter 4

DON'T CRY OVER SPILLED MILK

WHAT HAPPENS WHEN you wake up one morning and discover the person who you have been with for what seems like a lifetime is not coming home? MOVE FORWARD! This realization may be a slow, grueling process, or it may be like a flip of a switch. Whichever one you go through, it is no doubt tough! You have invested countless hours and energy into someone who, for whatever reason, is gone. It is important at this point to allow yourself time to grieve. Although the person is not physically dead, they are dead from your life. You must grieve in order to allow yourself time to get over whatever concluded the relationship. When I say grieve, I don't necessarily mean you have to go out kicking and screaming, although you might want to, which is okay; the point is to face reality.

The key is simply dealing with the fact that he is out of your life. This is not a time to beat yourself up with what he could have or should have done or what you could have or should have done. This is, however, a time to take inventory of your actions. This is really, really difficult to do, especially if your husband or boyfriend did something as bad as betrayed your trust. Most times we can't get past the question of, "Why did he do me like this?" We beat ourselves up for months and sometimes years asking this same old question and not getting an answer in return. These intrinsic questions hover over you because the wrong questions are being asked. At this point you can only speak for yourself, so you have to ask questions that can be answered and solved by you and you alone. Questions like: "Was I emotionally ready for this type of commitment? Did I ignore the warning signs up front and continue in what was already apparent? Did I lose my identity in this relationship? What did I contribute to this relationship? Was I helpful or hurtful? Did I respect him, his space, his ideas and his opinions? What was I truly looking for? Was I honest? Did I keep God first?" These are just a few questions to get you on the right path. The key word here is "I."

Don't take this as beating up on yourself, because it is not. This is a time to take responsibility for YOUR actions, for YOU! If you continue to try and answer for the other person, you will find yourself stuck in this grieving process longer than necessary. The real problem remains (untold); we don't want to ask ourselves vital questions directly. We are afraid that if we are honest, we might not like the answers that come back! We want to blame someone for our hurt, and that someone is unfortunately not ourselves. I hear you screaming at me: "HOW CAN THIS MAKE ME FEEL BETTER WHEN HE BETRAYED ME? I AM NOT THE GUILTY PARTY HERE." Sweetie, It's not about who is guilty at this point; the trial is over and the verdict is in — he's been proven guilty. The true trial is just beginning, and this is when you have to be truly honest with yourself, no matter how painful it may be.

I am not by any means letting those who are dishonest off the hook; it's not about them anymore. Remember, they're gone and the key is thrown away. What you need to be concerned with is how not to let this happen again, "What can 'I' do better next time, that 'I' didn't do this time?" I am not saying you will never lose a love again. I am saying that if you really look at your contributions, you are able to go back out on the playing field with a new set of rules and a new set of strategies to begin a new game as a better player. If you don't go deep and get honest with yourself, you will just go back into another relationship with your wounds bandaged. Under the surface your wounds are screaming that all men are liars and cheaters and not worthy of your love. You get involved with a new person because of the emotional needs, but emotionally you are not ready. You have not dealt with your emotions effectively and honestly. You are still looking at the other person's faults and not getting in touch with your own. It may not even be your faults that you need to get in touch with. It may be that you just need honesty in your life (from you about you), coupled with the understanding that you can't control someone else, no matter how hard you try! I have found that normally when you try harder than necessary, that's when things usually go bust.

My dear, you will find yourself spending a lot of nights alone and lonely; this is just part of the process you must endure. Trust me, I have been there, and it doesn't feel very good. Quite frankly, it stinks, but I guarantee you will learn more about yourself than you ever thought imaginable. It seems like everybody else's life is perfect and the bottom has just fallen out of yours. At this point, you can do one of two things — get better or get bitter. Unfortunately, a lot of women take the low road and get bitter. We start acting out our frustrations on the world because we don't think we deserved what has happened to us. We are hurt on the inside and we start being rude and nasty to anyone who steps in our path. For someone who has just met us, we are classified only as the "B." We may even get called this to our faces — or behind our backs. The sad part is we really don't care. We actually accept the accusation at this point. We are kind of like a skunk; when we get hurt, we put off this stink so no one will want to get close to us. What usually happens is we start to transform into this ugly individual by putting up a wall; however, it eventually becomes who you are. If you act out the part long enough, you become the part. At some point, we get tired of the stench and try to form sincere relationships, but no one seems to like the stench we put off.

Transforming into an evasive person only hurts you in the end because you don't allow yourself to form meaningful relationships. You don't allow yourself to meet new people because you believe they have an ulterior motive for wanting to get close to you. You feel like this because of your past hurts by people whom you trusted. You may feel like the best thing to do is wear your game face around with you everywhere you go, so no one will get any ideas of even attempting to get close to you. But what I have found is if you are honest with yourself upfront about who and what you want in your life (without being outrageous), you won't feel the need to put up a wall toward others. You have to get to the point of knowing the behavior that you can accept and what you absolutely will not tolerate in your life. There may be things from your past that you were not comfortable with, but tolerated simply for the sake of appeasing the other individual.

Oftentimes we put up walls because we know our weaknesses. We know how we handled certain situations or people in the past, and the results were not very favorable. There again, you must get in touch with what you "feel" you are weak about and try to replace the feelings of being weak to being self-assured. Being self-assured means having a firm belief in one's own powers. In others words, no one can do what you don't want them to do. No one has control over you and your life but you! You are able to take the good and the bad from people and move forward, making firm decisions as to whether this person is for you and your life choices or if you need to steer clear of them and their hazardous ways. The motive here is to allow yourself the opportunity to meet people and enjoy them to the extent they are adding something positive to your life and not taking something valuable from your spirit.

I know it's not easy after you have been hurt to move on with your life and act as if nothing has happened. Of course, that's not what I am suggesting, because that could be classified as denial and not getting in touch with your true emotions. I am saying work through your issues. Remember the number one rule: you have to go through your problems, not around them. This is where it starts to apply – start grinding at the problem. Get to the root of the problem, move off the surface where everything appears okay and move to where the anger and frustration begin to mount. Figure out why the frustrations continue to exist to the point of making your blood boil at the mere thought of the past events of your life. The only way you will begin to heal is by replacing the anger and frustrations with new thoughts and ideas, along with positive people and events. This can be done ONLY after you have pushed the pain up and out instead of pushing it down inside of you deeper and deeper. You will be doing the alternative at this point – getting better. Find ways to improve yourself. When you feel like you want to curse someone for doing something as simple as looking at you funny, say something nice instead. I know it sounds like a "yeah right" statement, but try it.

When you wake up after a long hard night of crying the blues because your babies' daddy or your future babies' daddy is not coming home, PULL YOURSELF TOGETHER. Put on a pot of black coffee if you need to and get up and get out! Pull your best dress out of the closet; do whatever you need to do to look your best. Trust me, at this point you are not going to care how the hell you look, but try it, and I guarantee you will feel great. People will begin to look at you and say, "Hey, something's different about you." Nothing really is different, other than the fact that you are "getting better and living life!"

To get back in the mainstream of interacting with people, start out easy by calling a loved one, telling them you love them. Keep the conversation brief, because if you talk long enough you will get drawn into talking about your issues, but call them to let them know you are still "alive and kicking." Get out into the world and enjoy yourself for a change. Go to work and be pleasant with co-workers or customers. Give a compliment to someone, so you are open to receive one. This is not going to be an easy thing to do when your life has totally fallen apart (or so it seems). So I am not even going to pretend that it is easy; however, life is what you make it. Remember one thing: “Joy always comes in the morning!” If you have to go home and fall to the floor every night to get the anger and hurt out, go right ahead. Just do one thing, and that’s get up in the morning and start a fresh new day. It may take 365 days (hopefully not) for you to fall out every night and get up every morning and start all over again.

One morning you are finally going to get it! I am still alive; this has not killed me! I am not even close to death like it felt. So you know what you can do at this point? First, you thank God for allowing you to have a sane mind, and then you start planning what you need to do to get your life back on track. You have missed out on a lot of precious days; fortunately, you have more good days ahead of you than bad days that have passed. After you have taken inventory of your actions and have gotten upfront and in your own face, you still need to sit back and relax for a minute. Sometimes we find ourselves so gung-ho to get into a new situation because we think we have done all the necessary homework. We think we know exactly what to do. We are like, “Let me at ’em!” But not so fast; slow your roll; pull your reins back; take it easy! Next time you go into a relationship, go into it believing that it is a million-dollar business deal that you can’t afford to lose. I can’t stress it enough: PRAY!. Do some research on your project (relationships). Look at other successful couples whom you admire and ask them their keys to success. Remember to take only what you need from them, because what works for some people may not work for you. More importantly, forgive people in your past for whatever wrongs they have done. Put it out of your memory. Take care of yourself, exercise, take vitamins and eat right. You need mental and physical strength to sustain the hard work ahead of you without quitting in the middle of the race. Find a hobby or something enjoyable that helps you release stress and tension. Step out of your comfort zone of things of the past. Be open and willing to meet new people and try new things. Venture out of your normal surroundings and maybe even your circle of friends. Last but not least, don't be impatient and go out looking for love. Trust me, you have a million-dollar deal (YOU)! Love will find you, so let it.

Chapter 5

Black Girl vs. White Girl

I HATE TO open this chapter up and come straight out of the box, but I must in order for this issue to be taken seriously. The negative energy that is used when a black woman comes in contact with a black man and a woman of a different race should this day forward be directed toward self. What is the number one reason a large percentage of black woman get so frustrated when they see a black man and a non-black woman together? Some black women are lonely, hurt, and, last but not least, want a black man for themselves. These same lonely and hurt black women can't understand for the life of them why they don't have a man and, secondly, how in the heck this woman has a brother seemingly so wrapped. Take a long, long look in the mirror and ask yourself questions to discover why you personally don't have a man, if that's your desire. Ask yourself this hypothetical question for starters: Who would you rather be with, a man who greets you with a kiss and a smile when you walk through the door, or a man who gives you nothing but attitude accompanied with complaints to last a lifetime? I may not be talking to you (that you know of), but drama is just a way of life for some black women. We have been conditioned for so many years to believe that we have to be feisty in order for someone to show us respect. It's almost like we have to prove that we are not doormats by giving much attitude to anyone who steps in our path. We especially display this attitude to black men; it's almost like we have to prove that no man is going to run our lives. This is totally a preconceived perception that black women in general have, because in most cases we don't allow a man the opportunity to prove they are in our lives genuinely to help us instead of hurting us. We just go into a relationship with this great big attitude, as if to say, "I am the baddest, so don't test me!"

We seem to carry this attitude around with us wherever we go, into the workplace, social settings or any place where we feel as if we have to guard our feelings and soften our emotions. People unfortunately do back off black women, but then a label is attached such as, "The black chick has an attitude problem." This label is not helpful; in fact, a lot of times it actually hurts us to the point we find ourselves lonely, simply because we are stereotyped as having a bad attitude and hard to get along with. I believe that if we need to defend ourselves in any setting we are very capable of doing so in a professional and appropriate way. However, we have a tendency to give someone a piece of our mind, and it's often not very pleasant. It is the need of some women to set the stage up front in order to set the record straight, but oftentimes this is very unnecessary. Other races of women usually don't have this chip on their shoulders, probably because they have not had to defend themselves quite like black women have. They usually take the relationship or circumstance for what it's worth, and that's a lot because the possibilities of any given situation are really unknown. Hmm! Women of other races usually go into a situation in an open and positive manner, actually eager to learn their new mates, environment or co-workers before they make a personal assessment. Woman of other races generally hold true to their bubbly, childlike personality until their mate PROVES to be unworthy of their love or their situations prove to be unfavorable. A lot of times they will try to salvage the relationship even after a bad situation has occurred by finding out what went wrong and work from there. A lot of times they will even ask, "What have 'I' done to offend you?" This is nothing more than taking responsibility for one's actions and finding a way to solve the problem and not make the problem worse. Keep one thing in mind: people are usually happier or easier to get along with if they don't constantly have to prove themselves or are not consistantly faced with confrontation. Whether it's about their self-worth, honesty, integrity, sincerity or loyalty, people like to be given a chance. A man likes to be given the opportunity to show and prove that he may not be like the last person you dated. Just as you get tired of running into the same type of people, well, this is probably true for men as well. Men may be tired of running into a black woman from whom they have to drag out the good and peel off layers of baggage because of what somebody else may have done to them in the past.

Another big problem with "US" women is that we put too many thoughts in our minds that are really not worthy of the time of day. We sometimes fill our minds up with beliefs that we cling to solely in our own imagination or past ordeals. We tend to make matters even worse than they are by acting on the thoughts and opinions we have totally conjured up. In most cases, our mates don't even have a clue where all of the drama is coming from. This can become boring and tiring, and some men simply don't have the patience to deal with a woman who has more than a little bit of unnecessary drama. I'm not saying all men deserve to be defended, but I know it is common practice for some women to take issues out of context and make a mountain out of a mole hill or turn a stream into a valley.

I want to share a few thoughts that I predict come into the minds of women on a regular basis. Take your mind off those negative thoughts for a minute and be open-minded to replace those thoughts with fresh new thoughts and ideas. We often think such meaningless thoughts as: "I only argue and complain because he's not doing what he should be doing" (according to whom?); "Being with a white women is a cop-out" (copping out of what, whose life choice is it?); "He's insecure, that's why he's with a white woman" (or is it really you who is insecure?); "She's trash!" (isn't your attitude?); "He cheated on his wife/girlfriend with me, so I know he is out there cheating" (first, you can never build your happiness on some else's sorrows, and secondly, why were you involved in an adulterous relationship with a married man?); "He's not answering my calls" (so this is grounds to badger and accuse him?); "He came home late" (has a crime been committed here?). Sometimes we mentally think problems into existence that are total nonsense. The above comments were pointed out to get you to see how we put so many negative thoughts in our minds without even thinking twice about how damaging they can possibly be and how these types of thoughts can control our behavior. We spend a great deal of our days operating with our minds out of control, instead of thinking positive thoughts or thinking of ways to improve our lives. We sometimes allow ourselves to sink into depression by letting our minds rule us. We drive ourselves crazy worrying about what someone else is doing and why he or she is doing it. This is one of the silliest things we can do – worrying ourselves to death about what someone else decides to do. What can we do about what someone else chooses to do? Nothing! If a man chooses to be with a woman of another race or any other women other than you, that is his choice. Why not just pray for their happiness so you will be blessed in return? Start knowing that blessing someone else is the only way for you to GET a blessing in return! Blessings don't come from thinking negative thoughts toward someone, regardless of their choices.

For so long women have been saying, "WE NEED ANSWERS." Well, simply put, these are the answers. It is not rocket science like you thought, it's very simple; you cannot control what another human being decides to do, so stop trying! The only thing you are responsible for is controlling you and your actions. Period!

I know there will be a large number of women who still cannot take the long hard look in the mirror and who will continue to fight the ideas presented. However, I think a lot of single black women are fed up with spending every Saturday night with the girls or, worse, alone or eyeballing a potential husband in the arms of a woman from another race. Take the opportunity to try something different and change your thoughts of destructive thinking. Move into thoughts that everyone should be allowed the opportunity to be proven innocent before being declared guilty.

Before we go any further, I want to clarify something so you won't tune the message out. Please understand I am not saying that any other race of women is any better than black women. I am saying that the actions of some black women make us all look unattractive and unappealing. Once a few black women are viewed as having distasteful qualities, we are then grouped as a whole, and that's when it becomes perceived that ALL black women have bad attitudes and are rude and nasty. People look for this sort of behavior from us and love to say, "See, I told you so." That's what a stereotype is, a preconceived belief or behavior. This is why a lot of black women feel they have been dealt a hand from a bad deck of cards and act out their frustrations accordingly. Some women feel like I don't have a bad attitude, but people think since I am a black woman we are all the same. From the very beginning of this book, I have pointed out that this is a book to make you take responsibility for SELF and not be concerned with what someone else is or isn't doing. Why give someone else this huge advantage over your life, blaming others for YOU not having successful relationships, careers, etc.? Stop pointing the finger elsewhere – at white women, black men, society, white men, other black women or whomever. Point it back at yourself. Understand that you hold the keys to your own destiny. NO ONE ELSE HAS THAT POWER!

Question: do you really agree with some of the

statements that are being made today about black men, such as, "All the good black men are being taken by white women or are in jail or gay"? If you do, you have probably contributed to the misconception by feeding into this theory. We indeed cannot deny the fact that a huge percentage of African-American men are in jail (trying to achieve the American dream of fame and fortune). This produces a great number of men sinking into depression and turning gay or living a bisexual lifestyle. However, there is still a GREAT number of men looking for lasting stable relationships. The key maybe is to look at men whom you have categorized as not being your type and getting to know the individual before dismissing them. The man who is with a woman of another race may not be for you, so why get upset? Set out to exert a positive attitude in search of a mate and keep your options open. We go out "LOOKING" for a mate with all these high expectations. We say they must have this or that (mainly material things), and if they don't have what we have proclaimed they should, we don't give them the time of day. Stop short-changing yourself; stay open to the possibility of possibilities.

Have you honestly read this chapter to the point where before you read it you were truly believing that the problem was out of your hands, but you now see hope because you see hope within yourself? If you do, we are making progress. Are you now open to trying something different — becoming a different person? If you are, I have done my job of getting you to understand some simple important factors: don't underestimate yourself, give yourself credit, more credit than maybe we as black women are receiving as a whole. There is no doubt that we have a lot of work to do to accomplish the goal of getting people to view black women in a different light. But if you are aware now of a problem and willing to make a positive change, that makes the goal much easier to obtain. This is simply a wake-up call for all those who still believe your man is destined for Susie Q and there is no one left for you, instead of believing that you are truly a queen in waiting deserving of a knight in shining armor.

Did you realize we really didn't talk a great deal about black women vs. white women, but about self? That was the whole point. Yes, this chapter is titled "Black Girl vs. White Girl," but it really should have been called "Black Girl vs. Self," for the purpose of discovering some of the possible reasons why our black men, or men in general, look elsewhere when wishing to pursue a relationship. It's not necessarily true what we have thought for so many years – that women from other races are naïve and that's what our men want. It has more to do with everyone wanting to be treated with respect, and men especially thrive off feeling valued and needed. You have to know your role, my lady, and walk upright in that role if you are truly seeking a lasting relationship. Negativity is a part of the problem, yet it only thrives when it has willing parties. Become part of the solution and change your attitude! We only have one life, you know the rest ...!

Chapter 6

CAN WE JUST BE FRIENDS?

IT IS SOMEWHAT hard to fathom that women and men can actually be friends and nothing more, but it's possible. I believe one reason why it is incomprehensible that friendships can actually exist outside of anything sexual between men and women is because there is such a physical attraction between the two. Men and women have different qualities and aspects that make them attractive to one another. We look at the opposite sex and our hearts start to beat a little faster. Sometimes we have even encountered individuals whom we can't take our eyes off and we are absolutely mesmerized by them. We may even encounter people who make us lose our train of thought; this is how we really know we are spellbound. A man may say that he loves to see a sexy and feminine woman, and a woman may say that she loves to see a sexy and masculine man. Whatever is being said and regardless of the deep attraction for the opposite sex, it is possible for friendships to exist beyond anything sexual. In some ways friendships of the opposite sex are actually healthier and somewhat productive in learning to improve relationships with your mate. If you are able to talk to someone and get a better understanding about the opposite sex, it often helps us to see a different point of view, a view other than what we are accustomed to thinking and believing. Based on the information our male friend has shared, we are able to go back to our mate and possibly make compromising resolutions.

It is good for men to be able to talk to women as friends because it isn't always easy for a man to share anything less than masculine thoughts with their male counterparts. Oftentimes, when men start to share emotions with some of their friends, they feel they will be viewed as wimpy or gay. This leaves bottled-up feelings and unattended emotions that ultimately become a problem within their relationships. Regardless of what we believe, men do have emotions; they are just trained not to show their emotional side for fear of being ridiculed.

It is equally important for women to have male friends. Women look up to men; we love their strength and their drive. Often fathers are absent in the lives of their daughters, who are left with only their mother's thoughts and opinions to guide them through life. Some women have never been around men enough to truly understand their emotional needs. Here again, we base our opinions on what a woman has shared with us about men and, unfortunately, a lot of times it's negative information.

If we are able to meet a man who can show us a positive male figure and maintain a friendship only, it gives us a different set of thoughts and opinions to work from. We are able to form positive opinions about men and in return live more peacefully with them. We gain a better understanding of their actions and not discount them as only being thoughtless and selfish sexual creatures. It is so important to talk to someone other than our female friends in order to get a different point of view. Often our male friends are able to be more honest and upfront about our sometimes distasteful lifestyles and actions than our girlfriends would be. Men don't tend to fluff things; they will usually tell us the real deal, and we are usually able to appreciate and receive their feedback on a friendship level, respecting their opinions. This takes us back to the fact that deep down inside we look up to men. A lot of times we are trying to find out what we are doing wrong in our relationships, and our male friends are able to give a male point of view and shed some light on the situation. Our male friends are able to tell us what men are looking for and what their expectations might be from a woman. Unfortunately, other women can't really help us here. How could they? They are not men and far from it. Remember the book, *Men Are from Mars, Women Are from Venus?* Well, this is true.

We are different, but how do you get closer to Mars? By getting closer to their species (MEN)! We have to learn what makes men tick and what makes them act and react, not according to our (women's) rules and regulations, but according to the laws of men. Women act on a different set of theories. What may be logical to you, unfortunately, may not be logical to a man. This is why it is good to have male friends without any intimacy involved. It is important to get a different piece of logical information to compare with your own in order to make sound and wise decisions. Once the intimacy begins in a relationship, I can assure you there will be problems. Help and understanding is needed at this point. Why? Because a new realm of emotions have just been entered. For example, you might not get offended if your male friend unconsciously didn't introduce you to another female friend at a party, but let your man make the same mistake, and he might as well have dug his own grave. Women take this as disrespectful and automatically jump to conclusions. We assume he must have an ulterior motive for not introducing the female; we don't take it as a simple oversight. On the other hand, our male friend can simply make an apology for his mistake and we have forgotten about it even before he closes his mouth. Our mate, on the other hand, will be hearing about the huge mistake from now until eternity. Why is there such a wide range of acceptance here?

Women are very territorial creatures. Once we feel our territory has possibly been threatened, we will go through all costs, even at the risk of looking foolish, to protect what we feel is ours. We don't want another woman to so much as smell what we feel belongs to us. This is where we make the first mistake; nothing belongs to you but you! Yes, he may be your man and you are his woman, but he does not belong to you and you do not belong to him; you are simply mates. Once you have this theory in your mind, that something belongs to you, you become defensive and overprotective and start acting on those emotions. This is where the trouble begins; your mate is no longer able to be himself (as your male friends can) without walking on eggshells. Your mate has to watch his every step because if he makes one false move, ca-paw-yaw – here comes the year-long arguments and the drama probably over something senseless and meaningless. This does not make for a very satisfying life — it actually makes for a stressful environment. Because you are in protective mode, you don't realize you're acting in an undesirable way, seeing nothing wrong with your actions. As a mother bear protects her cubs from anything on the prowl, women feel as if we are acting under the same premise. We continue to act in this manner repeatedly, not recognizing that we are scaring off our mate by this behavior. In order to translate some of the non-threatening behavior back into our everyday lives with our mate, it is important to maintain male friends — snapping you back into reality by possibly convincing you that your mate is not your possession!

On the other hand there IS a disadvantage to being friends with a male that can very well become hazardous to your relationship if you let it! It is VERY important to draw lines and boundaries. Some of the same reasons why men and women are drawn to just being good friends can ultimately be the same reasons that turn them into lovers. This is especially true if things aren't going so hot at home and your friend seems to have all the answers. Your friend may have a lot of the helpful answers because you ARE FRIENDS AND NOT LOVERS; that is the simplicity of it! You don't have to deal with one another on an intimate level, so it's easy to communicate. You and your friend may have such good charisma and understanding with one another that you may begin to feel a little more than just a simple attraction. One of the major reasons this occurs is because you are lacking something in your intimate relationship and you are yearning for more. You must realize where the attraction is stemming from and work on those problems at hand, being careful not to create other ones. This is done simply by gaining control of your emotions and getting in touch with what you are lacking at home. This is where the boundary line needs to be addressed, either with yourself or with your friend. You can continue your friendship only if you address the issues and deal with your friend to the point where you know your roles – FRIENDS ONLY! You must realize how and why you and your male friend became good friends in the first place and stay on that level. Most likely you trusted him and you were impressed with his character; he was easy to talk to and seemed to understand you as well.

The important point is, he didn't just understand you by chance, you allowed him to understand you. Nine out of ten times his mere suggestions about changing some of your bad habits or your lifestyle did not offend you. You actually welcomed the thought. If your friend happens to offend you in any way, you don't hold grudges. You voice your opinion with him, even if he does not agree with your point of view, and you are able to move forward and continue being friends. It also probably holds true that your friend seems to be there for you whenever you need someone to talk to. The likely reason this occurs is because he is not the subject of the conversation; he does not have to get in defense mode. Understand, it's easier to listen to someone if they're not the focal point of the discussion or if they're not the apparent "bad guy" who does no good.

Please, please understand that some people will take advantage of your weaknesses and play on your emotions. Again, you have to be careful about who you let into your inner emotions. It may seem like your friend knows exactly what to say or do in your time of need, but this could be a ploy to get closer to you. So be aware what type of relationship your friend has in mind. Keep these things in mind when you start to have a little emotional moment with your male friends. Continue to use your friend for the sole purpose of getting one step closer to Mars. If you see feelings starting to arise, nip it in the bud quickly. We already know it's a fact that women and men are attracted to one another by nature. God intended for the opposite sex to be eye candy; not so you could sample every piece, but for you to appreciate and cherish what you have. You have to come to the realization that you are a jewel and your mate needs to treasure and recognize your beauty, and vice versa for you. This is only done when we have the understanding of one another's characteristics. We need to grow in harmony with each other and face the fact that we simply have different points of view, yet realize that everyone's ideas count.

Did you think that for one minute I was going to let you slide in this chapter and not slip in how important it is for you to examine why people react in certain ways? Let's look at how your actions can determine or dictate an environment, affecting the situation in either a positive or negative manner. Sometimes it is vital to step out of yourself and question if you handled a situation correctly; excuse me, there is no such thing as "correctly," but "beneficial" to all those involved. Everything in life always goes back to you and your actions. In most cases, you either make it or break it. Being friends with a male can be very helpful to you in your personal relationship, but you have to know the role that your friend holds. If it seems like this could be hazardous to your personal relationship, you must cut the ties or simply cut back the level of the friendship.

One big problem with the world today is we want to feel good all the time, no matter the cost. If we get one minute of pleasure, that's the sacrifice we are willing to make. That's the easy road. But that's not the high road. Understandably, male-female communication is what we need more of in life, not another emotional roller coaster ride headed for disaster. Use your male friend to gain knowledge that's beneficial and helpful to you in order to produce lasting impressions on your life, impressions that will help you to make good judgment calls. Regardless of what you've heard, men and women can be friends without being lovers.

Chapter 7

DON'T JUDGE A BOOK BY ITS COVER

"GIRL, HE WAS really cool, great conversation and those eyes, but those sneakers had to go!" How many times have you listened to your girlfriend pass a person up because his shoes were run down, his car had a little rust or he was just not the right type? The list goes on and on with how women perceive men, only seeing the exterior or the "right here and right now" of them, instead of stepping back and taking inventory of their personal values and their potential. I am not talking about you practically changing a man to be what you envision him to be. I am referring to you listening to a man talk about his goals and possibly helping him achieve some of those goals, instead of waiting for him to call you for the next dinner date that you know he really can't afford right now.

This is truly one of biggest mistakes women make when picking and choosing a partner. Many women don't have the ability to look at a blemished diamond and realize that if they take the time to clean it up, it could be the best in the bunch. We want the biggest and the best-looking diamond the naked eye can see. The really good ones get left behind because we do not have the time to turn over a few stones and make true discoveries. This is just an analogy between men and diamonds, but unfortunately, the guys with all the glitz and glamour always tend to get picked up first, leaving the ones who are simple and humble behind. A lot of times the simple and humble guys are not given the opportunity to show what kind of qualities they possess. Instead, we hear women make statements such as, "Where are all the good men?" Women must get beyond looking at the outer appearance and be willing to go deeper to find what lies in the heart of a man.

We as human beings are conditioned to be dependent on one another for survival; this is one of the key reasons why men and women need each other. Unfortunately, more times than not, we find ourselves trying to live up to someone else's expectation of what they think we should be. We find ourselves trying to be perfect in the eyes of someone else.

Let's talk about perfection and how trying to be perfect or meet the perfect person gets the best of us and almost always ends in loneliness. Please realize that people are not perfect no matter how hard you look. No matter how appealing they appear, no one will ever be even close to perfection. God left perfection out of us, on purpose, I might add. We need imperfection to make us grow. If we were perfect, what would we have to look forward to in life? We would not strive to be God-like. If we can ingrain this in our thought process, we would not be so harsh on a person who does not speak perfect English or who does not live up to our every standard, and we wouldn't even look at the brother funny with his shoes leaning to the side. You never know, he may have walked a million miles and back. You have no idea the amount of knowledge he may have to share with someone willing to listen and give him a chance. Try to think positive about it and understand that the heart is what you need to be searching for. This should be easy for women because we are emotional creatures by nature, but we are missing it by a long shot. We do not have the time to go the extra mile to get to know the interior; our minds are clouded by the view of the exterior.

Unfortunately, we tend to attach a lot of emotions to everything we come in contact with. We want everything to be “beautiful,” “perfect” and “together,” before we are even willing to give it a second look. We do not realize how much we lose by not being able to get past something that was not on our wish list. If it looks like a little work, we do not want to get our pretty little perfect hands dirty. Let’s start simply. If we look at ourselves, are we perfect? NO! Never have been, never will be. So why is it that we have this belief that everything around us has to be perfect? The reality is that we want to be saved! We want somebody to pick up where our fathers left off or begin where our fathers never started. We self-consciously feel like we do not want to deal with somebody else’s problems because we have too many to deal with of our own. We feel if we attach ourselves to someone who appears to be perfect, they can transform our world into this perfect little haven.

Stop and think! How many times have you attached yourself to this “perfect” man who seemed to have the world on his shoulders, only to find out later that the world is beating up on him just as much as it’s beating up on you?

Now we have double trouble (that we actually thought we were avoiding by looking only at the exterior) because the man "appeared" to have it all together. The first thing that we must do is put down the blinders and come to the consensus that just because something or someone "looks" good on the outside does not mean they don't have a whole lot of baggage on the inside — "stuff" that is ready to fall out soon as the opportunity presents itself.

Women must stop and take the time to get to know what a man is really interested in and what is important to him, what his values are and how he feels about women. This information is vital to know upfront. Just like a book, no matter how good it looks on the outside, you always have to read a little of the excerpt to see if this is something you might want to invest your time in. You must read a little deeper into the first couple of chapters to see whether or not you made a good decision. Then after you have finished the entire book, you are able to prepare your final report.

Nevertheless, what happens to a lot of women is, they either do not pick up the right "book" (man) because it "looked good," or they put a "book" (man) down before they get deep enough to find the "plot" (heart). If a woman's attention is not grabbed upfront by something catchy to the eye, you almost have to start counting your losses. Women tend to be impatient and anxious, not liking the notion of waiting for anything. Women want what they want, and when they want it! I can say this personally and not be strung up, because I am a woman who has come to terms with admitting to not always being practical and patient. This is something that must truly be learned only by supplication.

When I say supplication, I mean you truly have to ask God to open your heart to "understanding things." "Things" that you are repeatedly getting slapped in your face with until you say, "Look I am tired of being slapped and not seeing it coming; I need understanding and help!"

Women do not see the slaps coming because they have their own agendas. When you have your own agenda, you cannot see the forest for the trees. Women just go on thinking, "I want this, this, this and that." When we think with our eyes ALONE, we always think we have found Mr. O.S. Right, instead of Mr. Ooh So Wrong. When we find Mr. O.S., we tell ourselves, "That was easy; I didn't have to do much work to find the kind of man I was looking for." Wrong, wrong, wrong and more wrong – too easy! Ending up at the same place at the same time – "There are no good men out there." No, you just were not willing to go the extra mile! Getting to the external is a requirement, not an option.

Women get instantly irritated when referred to as gold diggers or money-hungry, but in many ways it is easy to see why women are viewed in such negative ways. Women are naturally drawn to beauty and glamour; it is just in our nature. When something or someone is appealing to a woman, we tend to go after it a little faster and easier than something that has no pizzazz. The downside of this is that some women get caught up in all the glitz and glamour and start to make this a requirement for any man they encounter and may even start to pursue guys who "look" as if they have a lot to offer. Some women may even result in using certain physical attributes to increase their chances of getting what they want.

The result of this type of pursuit is almost never rewarding for the woman, ending in loneliness, brokenness, depression and low self-esteem because the motive was wrong from the start. It is important for women to interact with men on a level that will constitute self-dignity. Start demanding that men look at you and your fellow sisters with love and respect. What have we heard for so many years, but have somehow lost the true meaning of along the way? "You get respect when you give respect." This is truly a profound statement that needs to be a way of life. If we start looking at men and treating them as the intelligent creatures God made them to be, they have no other choice than to step up to the plate and act accordingly because God will not be mocked.

The same goes for women – if we start presenting ourselves as a respectable, valuable, virtuous woman, who can deny us of that right? No one is denying you from becoming the woman God created you to be, but you! The mission here is simply as entitled – stop judging a book by its cover. Stop being shallow and letting what you see through your eyes determine what you let infiltrate into your heart and mind.

One way of doing this is reading between the lines of what a man is presenting and what he is actually producing. Anyone can present a magnificent masterpiece, but what lies behind the masterpiece is what you need to be concerned with. Can the masterpiece hold up under wear and tear, or does it collapse under pressure? You will be confronted with this question as you start sifting through who needs to stay in your life and who needs to go. When you are not misled by the eye, you will find out quickly who and what you can believe, and you will come to know that a person can only falsify his heart for so long. When you look on the interior of an individual, you are able to determine the trueness of their character and discover their true intentions. Hmm, I know ... information to meditate on! It's okay, we will get there, slowly but surely.

Chapter 8

GETTING INTO A NEW RELATIONSHIP

"LIFE IS LIKE a box of chocolates, you never know what you are going to get." When we heard Forrest Gump say this, we just laughed and thought he was funny, but once you put a little thought into it, you realize the statement is really true. When you go into a new relationship, you really do not know what you are going to get. The same goes for the other person. You are not "Ms. Perfect," as you would like the whole world to believe. My friends and I call the new person you meet "The Representative." This representative acts on behalf of you; he represents that "perfect" person who would jump through hoops of fire if need be to get the potential relationship off the ground. "The Representative" holds "board meetings and press conferences" (fabulous lunch and dinner dates, followed up with bouquets of flowers to impress you). We all have experienced a new relationship where we feel like our newfound love has been dropped from the pearly gates of heaven right into our laps. Everything is going perfectly, and then about the sixth month, "The Representative" retires. Just as you have fallen head over heels, the real person starts to shine through, brightly!

Believe it or not, we ALL have brought The Representative to life at some time or another. We want to show a side of us that the other person will fall in love with and cannot think of living without. We want to be thought of as sweet, great, sexy, intelligent and any other word that describes an irresistible person. In my opinion, there is nothing wrong with wanting to be irresistible, but the problem comes when you can't live up to the standards that you have set forth. You have placed yourself in some tall shoes, and it becomes a challenge trying to keep those shoes filled. What happens is we start to get too comfortable; we feel as if we do not have to hold ourselves to the same standards that we have established. We begin to think we can say or do anything in the presence of our mate and not be judged any differently. We feel like we have gotten to know one another on a different level; however, there are two important points that you must stop and realize right here and now. If you cannot live up to the standards, do not start it. In other words, do not start something you are not willing to finish. If your true goal is to just be "Ms. Perfect" to get the man and to then drop the act once you got him hooked, STOP WASTING YOUR TIME AND HIS! Stop playing with his emotions; this is someone's life.

Some people may think differently. You may feel that once you have gotten into the relationship you just want to be "yourself." Again I say, don't start something you can't finish. Do not appear to be something or someone up front that you are not, later discounting your actions as just wanting to be yourself. If you truly wanted to be yourself, this would have occurred from the start and you would not have to explain your position because nothing would have changed; you are still you! Get it? You are what you get! Be true to yourself! There is nothing more time-wasting than getting involved in a relationship only to find out later that the person with whom you thought you were dealing is nothing like the impression they initially gave. Don't you agree? We seem to waste more time going in and out of relationships because we get so caught up on what "The Representative" has displayed to us. We get caught hook, line and sinker before we know what hit us, instead of taking the time to do a little background check on our new mate to find out who he really is.

Try taking things slowly for your own sake, and if your mate is not willing to slow down, maybe he is not the one for you. Also, stop blocking yourself from Mr. Right by continuously settling for any Tom, Dick or Harry who comes along and sweeps you off your feet. Remember the old saying: "Everything that looks good to you is not good for you." Live by this rule. Start setting standards for yourself and hold true to these standards. Walk with your head held high and keep a positive tone in your voice and know who and what you are at all times — A LADY!

Have you realized yet that happiness starts within? Regardless of what you thought or what your grandmother, mother, sister, cousin, aunt or girlfriend told you, it is possible for women to have successful, loving and fulfilling relationships. First, you have to keep in mind that you are what you attract. Whatever energy you put off, that is the energy you will get in return. You must also accept that some men are simply not ready for a commitment, no matter how much you want for them to be serious. It's not going to happen until they are truly ready. You must also accept that some men may never be ready to make the type of commitment "you" want.

Please believe that women mature faster than men. Women have their hey-days, and then we feel like, "Okay, it's time to settle down." A good number of women start to get into a rush to have a serious relationship because they feel their biological clocks are ticking. Some women think that if they don't get married by the age of 40 they are considered an old maid and no one will want them. This is so untrue. Women need to start knowing their value and demanding that anything less than respect is unacceptable. With all the reading thus far, you should be able to comprehend that the contemporary way women have demanded respect simply is not working. To be honest with you, in these days and times anything goes; we really do not have a clue as to what respect really means. Some women are desperate and will go through anything at all costs to have a man, get a man and keep a man — even if it means crossing forbidden lines to do so. We need to come to the realization that this is not good — understanding the lines of self-respect and holding ourselves accountable for crossing them for the selfish desire of getting our "needs" met.

I want to start focusing on what we need to do when we meet a potential mate and what happens after you have taken it slowly and established what is known as a monogamous relationship. We will walk on the journey that you must go through to sustain the fire of "relationship heartaches."

We already cleared the air on the repercussions of getting involved in a relationship with a false sense of character. You must go into a relationship openly and honestly. You must tell the individual what you are interested in, who you are, what you stand for and the direction in which you are headed. If you want to pursue a relationship, you should pretty much know all of this information up front about yourself. If you do not have a clue about who you are and what you stand for, this is not the arena for you. I assure you, you will be chewed up and thrown back to the dogs, and this is putting it mildly. I cannot express enough the importance of communicating up front what you stand for and hold true to your expectations. For example, if you have strong religious beliefs, make them known to your mate. If his beliefs are different from yours, he may not be the man for you.

Just follow me for a moment – if you tell your mate that you have strong religious beliefs and do not believe in sex before marriage, but only voice this after you have had wild sex and feel guilty about it, this does not represent your true character. Quite frankly, your character is looking pretty poor. How do you expect someone to respect you and your beliefs when it appears that you do not even respect them? You must know that your actions speak louder than your words. Your mate is not going to take you very seriously, nor is he going to respect what you have told him you stand for. We are all entitled to a few mistakes, but when you are constantly contradicting yourself, you are killing your character. Once you have assassinated your character, your mate has nothing to stand on and will do what he wants to do because he has no clear set of rules and regulations to follow. You are now fair game. "Let the games begin," is what he is thinking. However, once you tell your mate what you stand for and hold yourself accountable for your own actions, he will know right off the bat what you will tolerate because you hold true to yourself and your own words. He has no other choice but to take you seriously and know that you are not a toy that can be jerked around at any given notice. Your character now has credibility. You are not saying one thing and doing the opposite.

You need to know where you are headed – it is necessary to know your goals and the route you are going to take in order to achieve these goals. You need to have a game plan and a road map, so when you get off-track you can "mark your position," so to speak, and find your way back on the right path. Your goals may change from time to time, which is okay, but you need to make sure you include the changes on your road map in order to stay focused and on track. It may sound like a board game you are playing with yourself, but believe me, this is serious business. The road of life does get a little tricky; it is nice to have a companion with us on the long journey.

The key here is to be prepared for what you have ahead of you. Preparation will help to make anything successful. When you meet a new mate, you must share with him your goals and your aspirations to ensure that your life and his could possibly be a match. Who knows ... he may not be interested in going down the same path as you. Better yet, you may not be interested in the path that he has chosen.

It is important to know where you stand in a serious

relationship, instead of finding out that you are two different people heading in two different directions. Wait a minute! It is possible for two people to have two different goals, but you need to know if your goals clash or connect. This is something that you will only find out by communicating openly and honestly with your new mate. If you find your goals do have the potential to connect, be supportive of one another. Remember, it is not all about you from here on out. Both individuals need to be supported and need to feel a sense that their partner is behind them in whatever decisions they make. Be available to listen to your mate and help him solve problems, ONLY IF HE ASKS! If he does not ask for your help with solving his problems, let him handle them, but be supportive. Be a sideline cheerleader.

On the other hand, you may want your mate to be more vocal when you are experiencing problems or making decisions; you may even get upset if he seems uninterested. However, this is just the way some men are programmed. Men really do not know you want their help, or many times they really do not know what to say to help you. If your mate does offer a solution to your problem, be open to listen to what he has to say. Women have a tendency to get offensive and block out what someone is trying to say if they feel like they are not totally on their side or in agreement with what they are saying. We also have a tendency of not letting a conversation get started long enough to make a valid assumption of what the other person is really trying to tell us. We cut the other person off and add our two cents to an incomplete statement. We take bits and pieces of what we thought we heard and run with it. Often we are running in the wrong direction only because we did not LISTEN.

The key here is to stop and become a better listener. Listen to what someone is telling you. If for whatever reason you don't understand what the person is trying to say or you don't understand where they are coming from, make it known, ask questions (only after the person has completed their thought) to get a better understanding and keep the lines of communication clear. It is also a fact that in many cases women just want to talk about problems and really not look for a solution per se. This is different for men; they are used to offering solutions and fixing problems, not just listening like our girlfriends would. Unfortunately, men think it is meaningless to just listen without solving the problem — not women, sometimes we just like to talk. So trust me, if you just want a listener, it might be a good idea to talk to your girlfriend, or better yet, try telling your mate when you just want him to listen. This leads me to the next paragraph.

Be careful about who and what feeds your soul! I know it makes you feel a little better to call your girlfriend and vent when you have a problem, but sometimes this just makes matters worse. There are three reasons I believe this sometimes happens: firstly, this is probably your best girlfriend you are talking to, and more than likely she is going to be biased on your side because she knows and loves you dearly. Have you heard the saying, "every story has two sides"? Moreover, guess whose side you are likely to tell when you are talking to your girlfriend? Yours! It is just natural to tell how you feel things transpired. In some cases, you may actually be wrong, but because your girlfriend is your best girlfriend she leans to your side. Girlfriends probably will not really tell you your true faults because they do not want you to feel worse than you already feel.

Secondly, sometimes after you talk to your girlfriend you are ready to "kill a brick." You talk to your girlfriend and she goes on and on to tell you how she wouldn't have taken this or that, or how she would have told them to kiss her you-know-what. We have all heard this one: "Girl, you are better than me because if it was me he would be out of here."

Lastly, most times when you are finished talking to your girlfriend, has a resolution to your problem been found? Probably not, and you might even go away from the conversation more frustrated than before you started, because no real understanding of the problem was reached in the conversation. Again, nine out of ten times your girlfriend is not making you point the finger at self.

I know you are tired of me saying the same thing over and over, but at some point we must begin to look in the mirror and realize it's imperative that we make ourselves the focal point? It is equally important to surround yourself with honest friends who will perhaps help you search for relevant answers. We do nothing but hurt ourselves when we surround ourselves with friends and family who allow us to sweep our "stuff" under the rug. We are then allowed to sugarcoat our downfalls to the point where we are blaming everyone else for our problems except the one person who can control the outcome. Can you guess who that is? OURSELVES. "I", period! Unfortunately, we like these types of people around, because they do not make us deal with our issues. We tend to constantly make the same mistakes repeatedly because no one is being honest enough to tell us otherwise. Having and being an honest and sensitive friend is so important. When you have honest friends around you, they will let you know that you were wrong (when you truly are) and offer solutions to make matters better. You will learn to love and appreciate friends when they give you harsh but truthful information about YOU. You will also be able to return the favor and give them perhaps the same truthful information about THEM when necessary. In return, you both will be growing into better people! This is why I say you have to be careful about who you let feed your soul, because the wrong information going in can make hell on wheels come out!

Have you ever read the books from authors who practically call women ignorant to their faces? We rush out and buy these books that have titles such as *Why Men Cheat, How To Stop a Man from Cheating on You, Never Enough*, and the list goes on and on, but I cannot stomach it any more! These types of books are traps or trash, whichever you prefer, for women. We are so desperate to find the answers as to why men do what they do. Can I let you in on a secret? These books really do not solve our problems. Although these books are unleashing a lot of information, it is not the information that is going to help us women solve our problems. Are these books really offering any solutions to solving problems, or do they just make for entertaining reading, or do they just make matters worse? The books really just make you say, "Oh really?", "Yeah, that's true," or "Men ain't no good."

Now what? What do we do with the information that we have read? Most times we just go back to our mates and accuse them of something that may not even be true just because of what we have read in one of our books. We even go as far as saying to our mate, "That's how you get away with your mess," or we tell them how we're up on their tricks and games. The men continue living the lies because they can, only because we simply allow them to. We may demand change, but we do not change ourselves. When we do not change ourselves, men continue to feel that they can walk all over us as they have done time and time again. After reading some of these "fictional" novels, women just get better at snooping, arguing, or worse, playing the victim, because that's all the help these books provide!

I want to end on that note, because the last thing I wanted this book to do was turn into a male-bashing, we-hate-men book! This book is about changing yourself! Do not wait for someone else to change. How about you being the first to raise the bar?

These were just examples of things that can infect our souls and spread like cancer. We all know that once cancer is detected there really is no help unless you catch it in the beginning stages and treat it heavily. "Treating it heavily" in this case is done by placing positive people and things around you to "gut" out all the past hurt and anger. More importantly, try to prevent it from striking by knowing some of the possible causes. This can be a metaphor for our lives – once we start to let people or situations infiltrate our mind and souls, our whole person becomes infected. Once a damaging person or situation has entered our lives and has fed our spirit, it is hard to release this from our thought process, our actions and our outlook on life. Knowing this, you must be aware of who and what is damaging to your health (spirit) and stay away from any cancerous encounters that may cross your path. Better yet, you must be prepared for any cancerous encounters that WILL cross your path.

I can admit, and hopefully a lot of other women will agree, that there is a strong sense of, "As long as the other person is not changing their ways, why should I make an effort to change?" I have found that operating under these premises leaves you feeling frustrated; you are constantly wondering why you do not have a solid, meaningful relationship. The question is: what are you doing to change the relationship other than complain, fuss, moan and groan?

That leads me to women who ARE actually trying to keep their relationships intact regardless of the other person, but as soon as your mate turns his back, you start the complaining, moaning and groaning. This is known as backbiting, and I can bet your relationship is in shambles, right along with the women with thoughts of, "I'm not changing until he changes." You want to know why? You are not any better than the person who is doing absolutely nothing. You may as well be doing nothing because you are not getting anything accomplished. And my guess is that you are more frustrated than ever. Have you ever heard that God doesn't want your tithes if you have to moan, groan and think about all the things that you could have spent your money on, rather than your tithes and offerings? HE says keep it; it does no good! This is the same notion. Why make an effort to change in your relationship if your heart is unwilling and you are only making the changes to see what you can get in return? You should be happy with yourself because you are making the changes for you. It is up to the other person to realize that you are a jewel, and your actions along with your gestures say that you are happy within. Regardless of how foolish your mate may be, you still operate under the same theory: "I will be happy, do good and fulfill my promise, regardless of what the other person is or is not doing."

"You will not be changed or moved by anyone" – you really do not know how powerful this statement is. This is a mindset that women refuse to understand because it is so hard. All we think about is, "Shoot, I'm not going to let anybody run over me." I am not suggesting you lie down like a rug; however, if at this point you are still feeling a sense that it is about what the other person is or is not doing, I need you to go back to Chapter One and start all over. This time, read a little slower, and if you get to this point and still feel the same, start the book over yet again. It's meaningless to go any further in the book if you don't have the basic understanding down: it's not about what the other person/people/world is doing; you must know and realize this is for you and you alone!

Can you agree it is an understatement that relationships are by far one of the hardest things to master in life? Why is this so? People are different, and when you bring two people together who have been raised either in a single parent home or even with two parents, different parts of town, different religious beliefs, different age groups, you name it, the differences that people have can be a difficult situation to deal with. But the most important rule that you must accept in dealing with the differences is to never intimidate or ridicule your mate's ideas and opinions. Intimidating or ridiculing your mate is, unfortunately, one of the most hurtful things that you can do in your relationship, and will eventually bring it to an end. You must understand that a person operates the way they do only because this is what he or she knows best. It's as simple as that. We are conditioned from our birth through childhood experiences what our beliefs and actions in life will ultimately be. There are exceptions to the rule as with anything, but the bottom line is you act the way you do because you were taught to act in this manner. It hurts when someone comes along and tells you everything is wrong with you! You may see nothing wrong with yourself because you have gotten through life okay thus far. It starts to become a tug-of-war with you and your mate because you are trying to hold on to YOU, and they are trying to hold on to THEM. What you must understand is that something which may be as easy as A-B-C or 1-2-3 to you may not be the same for someone else.

The solution is easy – let a person be who they are. Ah, but there is a catch: make your life an example! Because although you may feel you are right and they feel they are right, I assure you that you both can learn a lot from each other if given the opportunity. Let me give you an example: the number one problem in marriages is finances. Your mate may not be as savvy in finances as you, because your parents taught you how to save, unlike his parents who lived paycheck to paycheck. If you go into the ring talking about how stupid he is when it comes to money, I assure you that you're setting yourself up to self-destruct on delivery. Try going into it with, "How about 'WE' try something different.

You handle all the finances for six months, and we will see how much money we can save. After the six months are up, I will take over the finances and do the same. 'WE' will then compare notes and work from there."

You can only imagine the end result if you are positive. This is just an illustration of how you must be smarter than your tongue, which on MOST occasions is faster than your thoughts! Be reasonable, not cocky. You may very well be able to handle the finances better than your mate, but let him discover this. You know the one thing that leads to the win in this situation is the part about not feeling intimidated or ridiculed. There are so many other examples on how two people can actually work together and not against each other, but I believe you get my point! Don't underestimate your partner; give him a chance to change.

Wouldn't it be nice to come home after a long hard day's work, after your boss has just worked your last nerve, to a hot bubble bath filled with rose petals with a glass of refreshing wine, dinner cooked, the children in bed, and a nice book by the bed? This is heaven (TO YOU!). On the other hand, flip the script — your husband had a long day and you say to yourself, "I am going to plan something nice for him." You unconsciously start planning the evening based on what heaven is to YOU! Your mate comes home to what took you hours to put together without any reation. I can see the steam coming from your ears. You want to know where you went wrong. You thought of all the things that were thoughtful to YOU and things YOU would have liked. Maybe all he needed was a cold one and peace and quiet through the ball game and then to top it off with you in a negligee.

We get so caught up on doing things that we like, but not taking into account that what may be appealing to me may not be appealing to him. A night that was supposed to be beautiful turns into sheer drama because you feel as if he is being ungrateful or uninterested. He may not be interested in taking a bubble bath with rose petals. This is a big problem, because we get hurt when we feel our mate is not interested in us. We start having negative thoughts about our relationship, and our minds start to wander off to the land of "no good men." You both start to bounce off each other's emotions and say and do things you really don't mean all because you didn't go beyond your personal thought process and tap into his needs. Making someone other than yourself happy is difficult, but the key is to be mindful of their wants and needs, keeping your ideas out of the picture. If you practice this theory, I assure you that you will have conquered half the battle, and I mean half. To be on point, you must take your mate for what they truly are – a real live, breathing human creature with emotions and feelings that must be checked and rechecked on a frequent basis in order to have order in the house, your house that is! Try practicing these points and I assure you that you will be well on your way to a happier and joyous union. Does life seem complex and complicated? Well, believe me, it is!

Chapter 9

Rejection!

HAVE YOU EVER been rejected? Of course, you have. We have all been rejected in some form or fashion at some point in our life. However, if you don't think you have, let me give you a few definitions of rejection so you can think again: to refuse to accept or use; to refuse to grant; to deny; to throw away; to decline; and simply "no". Can you say yes now? Rejection is just one of those things in life that, no matter how much we try to avoid it, at some point in time it will occur. Rejection is hurtful nonetheless. Rejection is so hurtful because it makes us feel incompetent, which in turn makes us question our self-worth. We begin to question what is wrong with me and why did "I" get rejected. Some people simply can't accept someone telling them no; they despise the word. While others just don't know how to pick up the pieces and move forward after rejection has occurred in their life. When you are unable to move forward, this tends to make the rejection all the more painful, because you keep reliving the fact that "I" was rejected. We don't generally use the word rejected; we oftentimes classify it as being hurt, denied or played, but when it all boils down, you were rejected. The bottom line is no one wants to feel this way; we sometimes even put ourselves up on a high horse to believe we can't be rejected. But no one is immune to rejection. The more you understand that rejection is something that does and will occur to the best of us, it's easy to laugh about it and say, "I guess that was not for me," and move on. Oftentimes we hold on to someone or something, hoping the decision will change. In the meantime, we are in a miserable state because we feel we are not needed. When we are in this state, we are easily walked over because we are vulnerable. We want things to go the way we hoped, and we will go to great lengths to keep the rejection from becoming a reality.

To be honest with you, when "control" as you know it has been lost, this tends to bother us all the more, sending our emotions off the meter. Some people go a little crazy when they can't control a situation. These types of people can be classified as none other than "control freaks." Control freaks generally try to build a rejection immune system. They tend to think they are better than someone else because of their financial status, skin tone, background, upbringing, hair type, eye color, education, etc. People try to ride through life thinking things can't and won't happen to them because of a box they have placed themselves on top of. When rejection and other life-altering events occur, it's painful because the mind has not been equipped to deal with unfavorable events. This is when many people start to question themselves with, "why me?" Once you start putting all of this negativity in your mind, you start sinking down into a bottomless pit of feeling unworthy, not understanding it's those "THINGS" happening in your life that MAKE you grow. The word

"MAKE" is stressed because if you were not challenged to grow, you simply would not. You're comfortable in "YOUR" little comfort zone and, of course, to you it does not look or feel as if change is needed, although everything else may be changing right before your eyes. As a child must one day put away his toys, the same premise happens to grown folks. What was good for you yesterday may not be good for you today. So sometimes God allows things to happen in our lives to set a fire under our feet to help us move forward.

When moving forward, we have to have a story (life lessons) to tell those behind us to help motivate them. Sometimes the life lessons are hard, but this is needed in order to grab and hold the attention of some. One of the funniest things about rejection is that once you have truly accepted the outcome and look back on "THE FACTS," you realize how much better off you are now that the event or person is a thing of the past. Can you admit this is true? I know I can.

One of the first and biggest mistakes we make is taking rejection too personally. This may sound kind of silly to say because you are, in fact, the one being rejected. So, of course, you're going to take it personally. However, I make this point because when rejection occurs we act as if we are the only one in life rejection has happened to and start throwing ourselves a pity party: "WHY ME?" People have been rejected from the beginning of time, and rejection will continue until the end of time; rejection does not start nor stop with you. The same as the sun rises in the east and sets in the west is how sure I am that rejection will occur at some point in your life. We cannot control another person's decisions. Sometimes we will go to great lengths to keep from being rejected, but ultimately we have no control over what someone else decides. We must learn how to soak up the big "R" and move forward. The key is to realize and accept the fact that rejection is just a part of life — a part that does not make us feel very good, but again it's just one of those things that does and will occur to the best of us.

There are several forms of rejection, but one of the most hurtful has got to be when your mate breaks it off with you. When someone tells you it is over, it almost feels as if your insides have been ripped right out of you. Unfortunately, breakups are very painful because more than likely your mate is the closest, most intimate person to you. You become frustrated and ultimately become bitter because you don't understand why this is happening to you. To add fuel to the fire, your mate has rejected you and moved on to a new relationship. This is when we have a tendency to start becoming irrational and not thinking clearly.

You may begin to plot ways you can get revenge because your emotions are tied to being rejected. The situation may even become a little ugly for all those involved. Even the innocence of children is at stake at this point because you cannot get hold of your emotions. As human beings, there is a strong desire to hurt someone back after being hurt. Oftentimes it is our belief that if we inflict pain on someone who has hurt us, this will somehow make us feel better. You want to make their life a pure living hell like you feel they have made yours. This occurs so often because there is nothing in the heart or mind to replace the hurt feelings. You do not know what to do to make you feel a sense of relief from the pain. How about doing something as simple as taking the high road and "SOAKING" up the rejection? Does this sound impossible or even ludicrous? I assure you, it is not. The saying, "Chalk it up to the game," applies here — "THE GAME OF LIFE." Can you imagine if at least one-half of the population could train their minds to deal with hurtful inflictions as learning tools? Do you know how much better off we would be if we were able to accept rejection? Cry about it one day and get on with life the next, without sending ourselves through unnecessary turmoil lasting weeks, months, maybe even years. It only works, however, if you can genuinely take something away from the ordeal to IMPROVE your life, as well as share the events with others.

Your sharing with and showing someone how you responded and dealt with the situation might help them deal with upcoming events in their life. You may be able to prevent certain life-threatening or hurtful situations from occurring in the lives of those around you that you love and care about. You will be able to touch strangers. When you don't react to a situation in an unfavorable or "expected" way, you will be asked, "How did you handle that situation so well?" It's all in training your mind NOT TO LET YOUR EMOTIONS GET THE BEST OF YOU. Understand, this is a learned behavior just like learning to walk and talk. You will not successfully have it under control just because you say you are going to do it. You will have to literally rewire your brain, which no doubt takes a lot of practice and prayer. Only through trial and error will you have successfully rerouted your emotions. You have to work at this behavior, because when you are dealing with "emotions," this is one area that you have little or no control over.

Another thing: you have to be very careful because changes do not occur overnight as you hoped. It is so easy for something to occur in your life that automatically pops you back into thinking and reacting to a situation as if you had never retrained your thinking in the first place. No matter how many times you think you have overcome a situation or a mindset, you have to constantly retrain your thinking by focusing on positive ideas, as well as surrounding yourself with positive people. It is equally important not to let outside distractions or frustrations hamper you from improving your mental ability in dealing with situations on an as-they-occur basis. You have to keep your mind sharp and ready to handle any situation in an intelligent and rational manner.

For so many years our minds have not been "trained" to deal with rejection or hurt. Women formed a learned behavior from their mothers, aunts or other females growing up. Some of the behavior may not have been bad, but I can assure you that about 90 percent of our learned behaviors were from an emotionally driven state. When your emotions are in the driver's seat, all in the way had better watch out. Our minds tell us, "this is what I am accustomed to doing because this is what I have seen and done so many times." It then becomes a mental learned behavior. Trust me, about 50 percent of the mental behavior that we have is not very good, because it derives from people acting on their emotions alone. I hope this is making sense to you because, whether you realize it or not, this is the most vital thing in your ability to work on "I." Period. Again, we have to be in control of our emotions and not let our emotions be in control of us!

The one big point I am trying to make is that emotions have a tendency to overtake us. If we understand this up front and start dealing with ways to curtail the hurt, it makes a painful event not such an earth-shattering ordeal. It's so important not to lose sight of this fact and to pick up the pieces and move forward in your life. Many times we do things out of anger that later we seriously regret. This unfortunately happens because of not being able to get hold of our emotions long enough to stop and think first before reacting. Women are frustrated for a million and one reasons, but the number one problem is that we simply do not know how to channel our emotions effectively. Understanding this is a starting point; the next step is doing something about it.

You must start putting the plan into your daily life routines. Beginning with something as little as someone not complimenting you when expected and you internally saying to yourself, "I know I look good, so that's okay if he or she didn't tell me so." Moving up to someone criticizing you and rationalizing it as, "I can take the good with the bad and move on" — on up to someone breaking off a relationship you thought was the real one, which is tough. You have to pick up the pieces and move forward with what you have learned from the relationship, good and bad, and realize that this was probably the best thing for you. If someone else can't see your self-worth, YOU have to, and walk in what you know.

Remember, E-V-E-R-Y-B-O-D-Y will be rejected at some point in their lives, but the true winner is someone who can hold their head high AFTER they have been rejected and keep moving without missing a beat!

Chapter 10

KEEPING GOD FIRST IN YOUR LIFE

THIS IS THE last chapter of the book, although it should have been the first, but as always I saved the best for last. I started writing this chapter at four in the morning when I awoke and said to myself, "God is so good and I am so unworthy of His love." HE has kept me even at times when I have been so disobedient to His commands and questioned Him as to why certain things were happening in my life. At a very rough time in my life, God told me to have faith in Him and He would handle the rest. I asked God, "What do You mean, all I need to do is have faith in You? I need more information." Imagine that, me telling God "I" need more information! No matter how many times I asked for more information, He never gave it to me. All I would hear is, "Have faith in Me and I will handle the rest."

During this rough time in my life, God stripped me of everything that I had known to be comfortable in my life. Everything that I had become accustomed to and took for granted was stripped from me. I felt like I was running naked in below-zero weather; that's what my life felt like. After awhile I had no other choice but to do just what HE told me to do, and have faith in Him. I let go of all my problems and told God, "Okay, since I must have faith, I give all my problems to You." I said, "Here, You worry," and from that point on I was no longer worried about how my situation was going to turn out. I was tired of being the pilot of my plane, the captain of my ship and the head of my house. I said, "GOD, here You go." I became the co-pilot, co-captain, and the wife of my life all at once. God had full control of my life at this point. Sometimes I would find myself trying to slide back to the driver's seat, but HE quickly informed me, "You don't run this any more." I would tiptoe to my corner and smile to myself and say, "You're right, I don't have to worry about that any more." I was feeling better than ever because I no longer had the worries on my shoulder.

I also understood this was not a time to just lie down and relax. Just like a pilot depends on his co-pilot for help, a captain needs his co-captain to assist him; and, of course, a husband needs his wife's love and support. God depended on me not to take this storm lightly and kick my feet up and say, "Well, I guess I'll ride this one out because God's got it under control." NO! HE needs you to be strong and ready to take an order upon any given notice. HE needs you to be attentive to the radar (your life) in order to make any necessary maneuvers. Most importantly, HE needs you to be willing to do HIS will in your life according to HIS plan and purpose. It is kind of funny when you think about it, because we really feel like if we do not run our life, who will? But excuse me, honey, I will be the first to inform you – God doesn't need any help running your life. The only help that He needs is for you is to be obedient, trusting, and stand steadfast on His word. I assure you that He has the rest under control. This is still hard to comprehend, and at times we all will find ourselves trying to run "our" lives because it is simply our nature. We automatically want things to turn out like we THINK they should, instead of trusting and believing in GOD. When the road gets a little rough, we say, "Oh, no, this is not the way," without consulting with the Head Man in charge. We just take control and get messed up every time. God will let you mess yourself up until you have no other alternative but to say, "God, I give!" God's purpose is not to make you or even allow you to suffer, but to move you closer to Him and show you there is no need for suffering if you follow Him and His route. We may ask, "Is this the way I am supposed to go?" It's okay to question your path, but only through lots of prayer and sacrifice will you find the answers.

The world we live in is so scary, and now more than ever it seems like women are getting the short end of the stick. It seems like all our hard work and sacrifice is in vain, but I assure you it is not. It is not God's desire to see women hurting, but for some reason women are giving up just when the fight seems to be getting good. Women feel like the struggles are too long and too hard, and we are not displaying the perseverance to press forward. We do not trust and believe that God will handle our precious lives as our grandmothers of the past did. Our grandmothers had confidence that God would see His way through any situation. Their prayers are why many of us are where we are today, and they are still praying for us. Women of today want everything exactly the way they want it, no ifs, ands or buts about it, and they want it now! Women do not want to wait for Mr. Right; we want to go out and find him ourselves.

We need to remind ourselves of the scripture, "A man who finds a wife finds a good thing." It did not say for a woman to go out looking for a man! We do not want to relax at home and study the word and learn who we are; we want to be out in the world taking a bite out of it before we even know what life is about. We have become disobedient to God's laws and are confused about our purpose. We do not want to listen to anyone because we think we have all the answers. We run ourselves wild chasing after anything that gives us even the least bit of satisfaction, even if that satisfaction is short-lived. We are undoubtedly tired of this rat race that we have become accustomed to.

I assure you this is not the time to give up; this is the time to stand up and fight and get back on track with what is right. It is time to satisfy more than that 5 minutes of pleasure, fame and fortune that we have been seeking. It is time to search after something lasting and fulfilling, that generations from now can talk about and feel proud of. Our sons' and daughters' lives depend on our strength and our willingness to stay obedient to GOD. Everyone has a different path they must choose to follow, but we all must follow God's path. When it is all said and done, will God be able to say to you, "Job well done, My good and faithful servant"? Will your children be able to look back on your life and say, "That was one heck of a woman I want to be just like her"?

I hope that you are going away from this book with a new sense of self, not a new sense just to change for a day or a month, but to make a life change. I once read that it takes a person about 20 times to read something or hear something to finally say, "Okay, I heard what they were trying to tell me and now I understand what I need to do to personally change." This is why throughout this book I have reiterated things to the point where you could say, "Enough already." There are chapters throughout the book that I know you needed to read about five times before going to the next. You must get the fundamentals down pat and become aware of your problems and know the things you MUST change before you can even begin to take the next steps into your future.

While reading this book, you will begin to understand why your life has stagnated; many of the outcomes that you will ultimately discover will hurt deeply to say the least. It is hard to give up that "security blanket," whatever that blanket may be. Yet it is important to understand the changes that need to made in order to move forward and be triumphant in doing so. I chose to put this final information in "Keeping God First," because life and understanding it is truly a struggle and challenge.

Without knowing and leaning on God, you will continue to go though life misguided, confused and misdirected. You will ultimately get frustrated and throw your hands up and say, "I give." But with God leading you and oftentimes carrying you, you will soon find out that life goes on with or without you, so why not take advantage and be a part of life. Live life to the fullest extent possible and enjoy every second of every minute that God has granted you because, remember, tomorrow is not promised. Be blessed, my sisters, and go forth in your journey.

And with the help of Jill Scott, we went out singing: "*Living my life like it's golden, living my life like it's golden, living my life like it's golden, livin' my life ...*"

TRUE PURPOSE

As one we are to be come for the purpose of fulfilling
The void that lies between us.
As your heart rests heavy on my body,
You become soft as a feather
When you ignite the flame within me.
The energy that you release with just being you,
No lies, no walls, no hidden agenda.
You come to me naked, unmasked and revealed.
The true being that you are,
The purpose of your existence is clear and conscious.
You heal my body and mind of all the past pains
That left me feeling empty and incomplete.
I once wandered aimlessly trying to find my way
In a world that lives by the saying get in where you fit in!
My mind, however, is no longer distracted by the thoughts
of: What am I to do? What is my purpose?
It's okay not to know is where I am today,
I will find my way out of the wilderness,
Because to know that you do have a purpose
Is to know freedom from wondering what that purpose is.
No longer shall I feel like I have to get there yesterday or
maybe even today.
I now have the energy to continue my journey on to
tomorrow.

The Lord sent you to hold my hand when I need flesh against flesh to prove to me this life is real; it is not a figment of my imagination.
He sent me your eyes so I could look into your soul
And see a part of the world that is missing.
He gave me the courage to stand strong against any trials,
The strength to use the courage
And the power to release the strengths within my being.
Knowing this all is why I still have a sane mind;
I thank the Almighty for that!
My mind is not as lost as many
And I am not so far gone to where there is no returning.
And on that note the only thing left to do is as we were always taught, "Look to the right and look to the left and then get going!"

About the Author

MELISSA McCURRY-PORTER was born and raised in Kansas City, Kansas, where she attended Our Lady and Saint Rose Catholic School. She realized early on that the Lord always had a plan for her life. While under the stern guidance of Sister Mary Susan, the values of hard work and a focus on life goals were instilled (no room for daydreaming!).

Melissa later graduated from Washington High School and went on to attend Kansas City, Kansas Community College, where she obtained an associate's degree in paralegal studies. With a desire for more out of life, she chose to relocate to Atlanta, Georgia. While attending Brenau University, she later decided to pursue her entrepreneurial goals with her husband as part owner of a staffing agency, a restaurant, and various real estate ventures.

Melissa has been blessed with a son from her marriage and currently works as a Licensed Real Estate Appraiser in the Atlanta metropolitan area. This is her first book.